Fiona C̄d̄

OWEN DUDLEY EDWARDS, FRSE,
Dublin in 1938, studied at Belved
see James Joyce's _A Portrait of_
University College, Dublin, then at the Johns Hopkins University in
Baltimore, Maryland, subsequently teaching in the University of
Oregon. He then worked as a journalist for a year in Dublin. He
taught in the University of Aberdeen for two years (1966–68), and
since then at the University of Edinburgh whence he retired in 2005
but where he still gives occasional lectures. His subject is History but
he frequently trespasses into Literature. He worked in the Yes
campaign in 2014 and found it like the Civil Rights movements he
knew in the USA and in Northern Ireland, the protest movements
against the war in Vietnam in the USA, Ireland and Scotland, and the
anti-Apartheid movement in Ireland.

with love

Scotland's Waterloo

OWEN DUDLEY EDWARDS

Luath Press Limited
EDINBURGH
www.luath.co.uk

First published 2015

ISBN: 978-1-910745-16-8

The paper used in this book is recyclable. It is made from
low chlorine pulps produced in a low energy, low emissions manner
from renewable forests.

Printed and bound by
Bell & Bain Ltd., Glasgow

Typeset in 10.5 point Sabon and 9.5 point Din
by 3btype.com

To three colleagues at Edinburgh University whom I can never repay:

Pat Storey, Tom Barron and Roger Savage

Contents

Timeline

10 April 1814

Lord Byron writes 'Ode to Napoleon Buonaparte'.

7 July 1814

Sir Walter Scott's *Waverley* is printed by James Ballantyne.

26 February 1815

Napoleon Bonaparte escapes from the island of Elba on the ship *Swiftsure*.

13 March 1815

The Congress of Vienna declares Napoleon an outlaw.

16 March 1815

William I made 'King of the Netherlands'.

20 March 1815

Napoleon reaches Paris and starts mobilising troops. Start of the 'Hundred Days of Napoleon'.

25 March 1815

Great Britain, Russia, Austria and Prussia, members of the Seventh Coalition, come to an agreement to supply 150,000 men each.

15 June 1815

Start of the hostilities. Napoleon crosses the frontier at Thuin near Charleroi.

16 June 1815

Battle of Quatre-Bras: Marshal Ney attacks. Death of Colonel John Cameron of the 42nd Highlanders. Wellington's Dutch army at an important tactical crossroads. It ends in a draw. Battle of Ligny: Napoleon uses the right wing of his army and the reserves to defeat the Prussians.

17 June 1815

Wellington's army marches to position at Mont-Saint-Jean. Napoleon draws his forces symmetrically along the Brussels Road.

18 June 1815

The Battle of Waterloo begins. Napoleon launches an attack against the allies at Hougoumont. Charge of the British heavy cavalry, including the Scots Greys and Inniskilling Dragoons. The French cavalry attack. Marshal Ney takes possession of La Haye Sainte. Arrival of the Prussian troops. Napoleon despatches the elite Imperial Guard, but they are defeated. The Prussians storm Plancenoit and the French armies disintegrate. The battle is won by the allied forces.

24 June 1815

Napoleon announces his second abdication.

8 July 1815

Louis XVIII returns to Paris to reclaim the French throne.

28 July 1815

Sir Walter Scott sets out for Waterloo.

15 July 1815

Napoleon finally surrenders to Captain Frederick Maitland of the HMS *Bellerophon*.

9 August 1815

Sir Walter Scott arrives at Waterloo.

15 October 1815

Napoleon disembarks on the island of St. Helena, where he is henceforth to stay in exile.

23 October 1815

Sir Walter Scott's 'The Field of Waterloo' is printed by James Ballantyne.

20 November 1815
The *Treaty of Paris* is signed.

3 May 1816
Lord Byron arrives at Waterloo.

16 September 1816
Lord Byron's *Childe Harold's Pilgrimage*, Canto III is printed by John Murray.

1816
Charles Bell's *Surgical Observations* is published.

5 May 1821
Napoleon dies and is buried on the island of St Helena.

1822
Commissioned by the Duke of Wellington, David Wilkie paints *Chelsea Pensioners Reading the Gazette of the Battle of Waterloo*.

1881
Elizabeth Lady Butler paints *Scotland Forever!*

December 1894
The first of Arthur Conan Doyle's Brigadier Gerard stories, 'How the Brigadier Won His Medal' is published in the *Strand* magazine.

Preface

To work out the importance of Waterloo for Scotland confronts the historian with the 19th-century hostility to Scottish identity surviving the Union for any purposes other than tourist enhancement, military recruitment, picturesque costume, drawing-room singing, Presbyterian piety and Queen Victoria's affection for her manservant John Brown (1826–83).

Where Scottish history was permitted to exist, it was firmly closed with the Union of 1707. Peter Hume Brown (1849–1918) was appointed the first Professor of Scottish History at Edinburgh University in 1901 and had already begun his *History of Scotland* (published between 1899 and 1909). His candidacy for the Chair of History at that university had been set aside for less qualified but more English applicants in 1894 and 1899 but a legacy had forced the Sir William Fraser Chair of Scottish History into existence. He at least saw that Scotland had continued to exist historically, and weighed in on Waterloo with the evidence from perhaps the wittiest Scottish memorialist of the time (*History of Scotland*, III. 400):

> According to Lord Cockburn, the year 1815 – the year of Waterloo and the fall of Napoleon – divided in twain the lives of his generation. Previous to that year the double dread of revolution and invasion had been fatal to all reform; when that dread was removed, the nation could breathe more freely and with new-born confidence turn its thoughts to political and social amelioration.

He added a thoughtful footnote:

> A story is told of James Mylne, Professor of Philosophy at Glasgow and an ardent Reformer, which illustrates the tension of public feeling. On Sunday 26 March 1815, news came of Bonaparte's escape from Elba. Preaching that day, in the University Chapel, Mylne gave out the paraphrase, beginning, 'Rejoice! He comes, your leader comes!' This was interpreted as a

welcome to Bonaparte, and Mylne was prosecuted by the Lord
Advocate.

Hume Brown nevertheless noted little immediate change in poverty
of the lower class and repression from the upper. Henry Cockburn
(1779–1854), a Whig remembering the growth of Whig sentiment
in the 15 years before the Whig return to power of 1830, had
been more optimistic (*Memorials of His Times* (1909 [1856],
269–9):

> In 1814 the Allies made their first conquest of Paris, and for a year
> Europe was without Napoleon. Hostilities were unexpected
> renewed in 1815, and then ceased, after the short and brilliant
> flash at Waterloo; but in 1814 a war which had lasted so long that
> war seemed our natural state was felt to be over...
>
> Meanwhile a generation was coming action so young that its mind
> had been awakened by the excitement of the French revolution,
> and not so old as to have been put under a chronic panic by its
> atrocities... The force of this new power was as yet unknown, even
> to those among whom it was lodges, particularly in Scotland.
> Nowhere in this part of the [United] kingdom, expect at Edinburgh,
> was there any distinct scheme, or rational hope, of emancipation.
> But the mind of the lower, and far more of the middle, classes had
> undergone, and was still undergoing a great, though as yet a silent
> change, which the few who had been long cherishing enlightened
> opinions lost few opportunities of promoting and directing.

Was this to argue that the Enlightenment (nowadays too easily
taken to have ended with the Revolutionary and Napoleonic wars)
was in a serious educational sense begun after them? Or that in
Scotland it had survived them? That last would certainly be true
in Medicine.

A more direct sense of Scotland as product of Waterloo was
still being offered in 1902 from the Reverend James Mackenzie's
The History of Scotland, originally published in 1867 in the high
tide of imperial rejoicing after the eradication of Indian Mutiny.
It duly ended at the Union but with a bright afterglow for
Scotland (pp. 657–59):

From the period of the Union, Scotland, amalgamated with England into one empire, ceases to have a separate history...

And where is the region of the earth in which Scottish blood has not flowed to maintain the rights and honour of Britain? The snows of Canada and the sands of Egypt, the fields of Spain and of India, have drunk it in. The ringing cheer of 'Scotland for ever!' as the Greys galloped down the slope of Waterloo, told that the despot's hour had come. And who will ever forget the 'thin red streak' at Balaclava, or the battle march of Havelock's men to the relief of Lucknow?

The sense of the Union as proto-Dracula for a sacrificial Scotland might be less evident to less elevated souls than his sanguinary Reverence, but his symbolics are instructive. Balaclava was a British disaster, the Indian Mutiny (however answered by 'The Campbells are Coming') an indictment of British misgovernment of the UK's own troops, but undoubted proof that to proclaim defeat as victory is the recipe for success. (To do the British justice, they saved the world by that response to Dunkirk).

The leading professional historian of our own day, Professor Sir Thomas Devine, uses such sentiments to tempt readers of his *Scotland's Empire* (2003) but as meat for the student rather than for the patriot (pp. 356–8):

This enduring association between militarism, Scottishness and Britishness came relatively late in the 18th century. Highland levies, all exempt from the post-'45 ban on Highland dress, had fought with distinction during the Seven Years War and the American War of Independence. But they only became icons of national valour during the Revolutionary and Napoleonic Wars...

It was their role in three famous victories between 1799 and 1815 which transformed the Black Watch and the other Highland regiments into national celebrities... the Cameron Highlanders, the Gordon Highlanders and the Black Watch all distinguished themselves at Waterloo. *The Times* praised their bravery and elan while the three regiments also received the battle honour 'Waterloo' on their colours.

And the late Professor Rosalind Mitchison (1919–2002) showed how religion reflected Waterloo in ways a Churchman of Scotland like Mackenzie might have noted:

> The new post-Napoleonic state was very different from miscellaneous collections of privileges and exemptions which had constituted the political structures of the 18th century... The relations of all established churches to the newly effective government power had to be defined and redefined as the governments increasingly accepted the principles of popular representation. Churches and states were both claiming increased authority on territory they had hitherto shared. (*A History of Scotland* (2002 [1970] 384.)

It might seem a long way from Waterloo to the Disruption of the Church of Scotland in 1843, but Rosalind Mitchison's argument implicitly carried with it the reminder that Napoleon (1769–1821) and his Papal Concordat took direction of a new agenda for religion and its uses for the state. Rulers had been trying to conscript religion to their advantage since before recorded history, but here as elsewhere Napoleon modernised rationally if tactlessly, and when Waterloo removed him definitely and finally his victors had to make the most of the world he had remade.

Alex Salmond, in his memoir of the Scottish Referendum of 2014 *The Dream Will Never Die* (2015), opined that Prime Minister David Cameron 'believed the centenary of the Great War in 2014 would be of... significance in reminding Scotland of the glory of the union'. Mr Salmond is probably right. The subsequent completion of Mr Cameron's first administration and his consequent re-election would seem to have vindicated my thesis that Mr Cameron is far more intelligent than he sounds, but the notion that patriotism (vote-gathering or otherwise) climaxes in rejoicing at violence is certainly an old Tory superstition. Margaret Thatcher (1925–2013) as a parvenue was desperately anxious to prove her high Tory credentials, and consequently told media reporters to 'Rejoice' at some success in the Falklands or Malvinas War. It exhibited an odd interpretation of the purpose and nature of pressmen, but it certainly was a traditional Tory strain. The Victorian Music-Halls, appropriate antecedents of Thatcher chauvinism, expressed it in 1877–78 at the prospect of war with Russia:

We don't want to fight, but, by Jingo, if we do,
We've got the guns, we've got the men, we've got the money too...

although even that baptism of Jingoism began by denying a desire to fight. And 'Jingo' never really became indigenous to Scotland albeit we were informed by *The Chambers Dictionary* (before it became a mere Hachette job) that its less ideological derivative 'Jings' did (particularly in the world of *Oor Wullie*). The equation of patriotism and bellicose intent is common to many other cultures. Violent Irish nationalism (whether Orange or Green) is in many ways the child of British chauvinism, and refuelled itself with many songs on alleged Irish provenance of masculinity by sanguinary aspirations (from 'The Sash My Father Wore' to the Irish national anthem). Irish constitutional nationalism bootlegged folksong expressions of this, but in sobriety it was constructive, furthering the massive extension and organisation of democracy in these islands during the Irish Union with Britain, particularly under the leaderships of Daniel O'Connell (1775–1847) and Charles Stewart Parnell (1846–91).

Mr Salmond went on to assert that Mr Cameron's conviction that war nostalgia would determine the outcome of the Referendum debate, 'betrayed a huge misunderstanding of the Scottish psyche. As a martial nation Scots tend to revere soldiers but oppose conflict'. I only read this after writing the present book, and I certainly was not trying to prove it. But having completed my researches and written the results, it looks very much to me as though Mr Salmond was right about Waterloo. I started out, at the request of that midwife extraordinaire, Mr Gavin MacDougall of Luath, to find out what Scots thought about Waterloo, and what I kept on finding was a sense of horror. This sense of horror was there whether the writers had witnessed the battle in 1815 or simply visited the terrain within the next few months, and this sense of horror was there no matter how great Scots' admiration for the courage that the Scottish soldier displayed.

It was obvious enough that few Scots were likely to share English consciousness of war against the French as a national heritage. It doesn't mean they were likely to make that much of the Scottish historical identification of national war as usually entailing a French alliance. Rudyard Kipling (1865–1936), propagandising to the Irish in 1914, said they would be 'fighting for France again', knowing as he did that 18th-century Irish military glory had been chiefly limited to service in continental armies during prohibition of Irish Catholic recruitment in British service. (Kipling loved the Irish, making several of his heroes Irish, notably Kim.) The Scots were officially expected under the Union to have performed the change of military sides in 1748–56, when Britain switched from Austrophile to Prussophile, so that Jacobite Scots would ease from Francophile to Anglophile. Enough of them performed this nominal transfer of loyalties for it to be taken as successful. But Waterloo ceremonially set the capstone on Britain and Ireland (the new United Kingdom born on 1 January 1801). Sir Walter Scott (1775–1832) in some ways a historiographical security risk for earlier times, affirms in these pages Waterloo as the expression of UK military identity. The invaluable multi-authored *Military History of Scotland* edited by Jeremy Crang, Edward Spiers and others (2014) shows us a much more complicated past than that but would have to concur in its ambiguity as well as its complexity. 'Scotland Forever!' was a Waterloo war-cry, but it implies a living people.

The memory of Waterloo is no more likely to promote feelings of insular (or archipelagan) solidarity than is that of the Great War. It deserves recognition as a British moment, within which Scottish self-expression was ready to proclaim itself. There is a strong British tradition which asserts hostility to Waterloo perhaps most memorably in the verse of Hilaire Belloc (1870–1953) and G.K. Chesterton (1874–1936). Belloc's 'Ballade of Unsuccessful Men' saw the Devil as hostile to 'The cause of all the world at Waterloo', meaning the cause of Napoleon, partly from Belloc's wish to think himself French. Chesterton's 'The Secret People' (recently if ludicrously quoted in the 2015 General Election by Scotophobe Tory propagandists) made more English sense although ending in the same rejection of Waterloo as a victory for Britain:

In foam and flame at Trafalgar, on Albuera plains,
We did and died like lions, to keep ourselves in chains
We lay in living ruins; firing and fearing not
The strange fierce face of the Frenchmen who knew for what
    they fought,
And the man who seemed to be more than man we strained
    against and broke;
And we broke our own rights with him. And still we never
    spoke.

Chesterton was Scottish enough to withdraw from a Glasgow University Rectorial election in favour of the Scottish Nationalist candidate, and to love Walter Scott, but there was nothing particularly Scottish in this rejection of Waterloo.

Chesterton in fact summed up English resistance to Napoleon in his novel *The Flying Inn* (1914) where outlaws in a motor car invent songs to explain 'the rolling English road' the paradox of whose virtue is declaimed by a Wildean aesthete named Dorian Wimpole;

I knew no harm of Bonaparte and plenty of the Squire,
And for to fight the Frenchman I did not desire;
But I did bash their baggonets because they came arrayed
To straighten out the crooked road an English drunkard made...

But the modernisation he saw as inevitable should Napoleon have realised his lifelong ambition to conquer England had already been imposed on Scotland, by enlightened Scots and by Anglicised clan chieftains. The poem won its Britishness when the English drunkard in the ditch under a wild rose inspired Hugh MacDiarmid aka Christopher Murray Grieve (1892–1978) to proclaim modern Scottish nationalism in *A Drunk Man Looks at the Thistle* (1925)

If this book had been somewhat bigger it would have contained Scots' retrospective visions of Waterloo. Thomas Babington Macaulay (1800–59) was Leicester-born and London-reared, but as the son of a Gaelic-speaking Highlander/Islander he sometimes identified with the historic bards, and about 1824 he produced a hilarious parody of the plot of Virgil's *Aeneid* in 'The Wellingtoniad', imagining a version of Waterloo by a poet of the remote future with Gods and heroes of the classical kind whether genuinely Homeric or artificially Virgilian. It was lively and even bawdy enough, with Virgilian-style Funeral Games winning a prize of 12 opera girls for the Duke of Wellington (which in real life he might have been ready enough to welcome). This did not reject Waterloo, but it was ready mildly to mock the Tory hero increasingly identified with the reactionary government. Arthur Conan Doyle (1859–1936) was the great short story-teller of Napoleonic history, his Gerard stories unrivalled as a historical fiction series, of which a linked pair show how the comic heroic French soldier bore himself at Waterloo, while his short story 'A Straggler of '15' (1891) about the last days of an old English soldier remembering Waterloo decades later became a great stage success starring Henry Irving (1838–1905) and renamed 'Waterloo' (1894–95). Conan Doyle's achievement in visualising the Napoleonic wars from a devoutly Napoleonist viewpoint is particularly remarkable. He himself was a devout Unionist (though one converted to Irish Home Rule) and his Irish parentage and Scots birth and upbringing seem to have given him the detachment necessary to make a successful narrator and protagonist of Gerard. As it is, the present book largely restricts literature to perhaps the most interesting literary witnesses of the battle. And since Scottish medicine in 1815 was probably the best in the world, we have medical authorities as well as soldiers among our authors. Their work is officially non-fiction although any memoir of a battle will contain some fiction whether the authors realise it or not. Our soldiers include two sergeants, who have enough command to see more of the battle than their immediate surroundings, but not enough to lose touch with humanity. We have also one soldier whose existence, let alone his narrative, has been questioned, but if Howell is more fictional than the rest, whoever perpetrated him understood and probably witnessed Waterloo.

Our intention then was to discover what the Scots made of Waterloo, but to do so through writers whether participants in the battle or not. Neither Gavin MacDougall nor any of his admirable staff nor I had any initial thesis to prove or disprove. We were neither caught up in fundamentally racist assumptions about a Scottish propensity for killing fellow-humans nor a denial of readiness to fight on the part of those who fought or who celebrated it. We were particularly anxious to get Walter Scott's findings and expression of them into our narrative, and thus knowing that his chief prose work *Paul's Letters to his Kinfolk* was to be reprinted we turned to his letters to his wife and other correspondents, as well as taking a fresh look at his 'The Field of Waterloo'. Byron his friend naturally followed, and while I knew they really liked one another, I had not realised how similar in some ways their responses could, regardless of political differences between two men so passionate in political expression so affectionate in indifference to their differences. We have concentrated on a few witnesses considered in detail but have taken soundings from many other contemporaries. We found that Waterloo forced attention to Scots' political and constitutional attitudes and that here much more than elsewhere was a British consciousness. Just as we could say of the Battle of Britain, the Union was intensely alive there, in a different form the same seems possible to perceive of Waterloo.

But while we may be refreshed by the thought of Scots finding new directions whence to look at themselves and their neighbours in the archipelago and Union, we must remember what discussions of such great battles so often miss, the unfortunate locality where they happen. *1066 And All That* opens up new ways of wisdom whenever we look at its hilarious pages, certainly including its remark that the first World War was between America and Germany and was thus fought in Belgium. Belgium seems forever caught between the pass and fell incensed points of mighty opposites, but if the Scots might have understood better what it meant to be Scots while thinking of Waterloo, what did it mean to the people amongst whom, and to whom, so much of it happened? How many discussions of Waterloo even think of the fact that 15 years later Belgium would come into political existence following a successful revolt against the new Kingdom of the Netherlands to whom the victors in the Napoleonic wars had consigned the southern Netherlands? And for all of the Waterloo conquerors' anxiety to obliterate the French Revolution the Belgians would achieve their independence partly through the Roman Catholic clerics who had been so hostile to the French revolutionaries. If Scotland thought back on its days of independence, Belgium had 2,000 years of conscious identity as the victim of some great powers, the football of others. In our book we keep on running into references to Belgium and the Belgians which first seemed anachronistic and became clearly unavoidable. After all, Caesar's *Gallic Wars* in their second campaign (or Book) had featured the Belgae in a big way, and his incursion to Britain partly arose from British-Belgian links (it is a pleasant thought that Brussels (or its ancient and medieval equivalents) is one of the oldest points of diplomatic and demographic reference in British history).

You are in many different hands in this book, and it seems sensible to stress Scott's incredible value as a historical witness whether through observation, imagination or wisdom. I don't add a regret that nobody reads him now, so often repeated, and so untrue. Writers on Scott however valuable have been saying this for the last century, regardless of the fact that so many of his works have been on sale during that time, and that publishers are neither sentimentalists nor philanthropists.

It only remains for me to thank my admirable publishers, particularly Gavin MacDougall and Chris Kydd, and to thank even more deeply and passionately the National Library of Scotland all of whose staff are invariably so wonderful to me and encouraging in my literary enterprises. I am deeply grateful to my colleagues and students, in English and Scottish Literature, Scottish

Studies and Politics, and in history of every shape and kind, at the University of Edinburgh. As in so many historical enterprises, I am deeply grateful to Pat Storey for her unstinting aid and infectious enthusiasm. I must also thank Edinburgh University Library, Edinburgh Central Library and the National Library of Ireland. And I cannot thank my family enough, above all my wife Bonnie, without whom my life would have been an endless series of Waterloos.

Introduction

The Reverend George Robert Gleig (1796–1888) was a Scot with a military record, followed by ordination as a Scottish Episcopalian minister (his father George (1753–1840) was Bishop of Brechin). The younger George Gleig served in the Napoleonic wars, was wounded, and became a priest in 1820, ultimately combining both of his professions by appointment as chaplain-general of the forces (1844–75). He wrote extensively for Scottish or Scottish-influenced magazines – the *Edinburgh Review*, *Blackwood's*, the *Quarterly Review*, *Fraser's* – and also produced many books. His biographies were stalwart crusades defending their subjects, sometimes questionably. Thomas Babington Macaulay reviewing his volumes on the administrator of India Warren Hastings (1732–1818) wrote 'It is not too much to say that Mr Gleig has written several passages, which bear the same relation to the "Prince" of Machiavelli that the "Prince" of Machiavelli bears to "The Whole Duty of Man", and which would excite amazement in a den of robbers, or on board of a schooner of pirates', a verdict which evidently inspired W. S. Gilbert (1836– 1911) to make the pirate king in *The Pirates of Penzance* (1879) assert his moral superiority to legally appointed rulers. Gleig was not inclined to ask awkward questions of his heroes.

Inevitably Arthur Wellesley (1769–1852), Duke of Wellington, was one of them. Gleig had served under Wellesley's command in the Peninsular Wars but having been sent for service in the War of 1812 against the United States of America, Gleig missed Waterloo and never quite got over it. His book *The Story of Waterloo* appeared in 1847, his biography of Wellington in 1862, and when (at the same age as the present writer) he produced his *History of the Reign of George III to the Battle of Waterloo, with Outlines of Literature during the Period* (1873), clearly intended for the use of schools, he intended to do Waterloo proud. Having shown Napoleon abdicating and being given the toy kinship of the island of Elba, he first noted the premature rejoicings in 1814 for the advent of an apparently lasting peace, and then ushered in Waterloo. We are concerned with the way some Scots thought about Waterloo whether they had participated in it or not, and we will let the regretful absentee be the first one to talk to us about it (pp. 120–23):

> ... England was the scene of festivity and rejoicings, such as had never before been witnessed. The allied sovereigns, the Emperors of Austria and Russia, and the King of Prussia, with the most distinguished of their nobles and officers, visited London, and the whole mass of the population appeared giddy with delight. In both Houses of Parliament, likewise, the Duke of Wellington [for he had been raised, by a grateful prince [the future George IV (1762–1830 Regent 1811–20 rgd 1820–30)] to the highest dignity of the peerage] was hailed, both by the Lords and Commons, with enthusiasm; while the people out of doors appeared almost willing to cast themselves under his chariot-wheels.

> In the midst of all this triumph, however, the allied sovereigns did not suffer themselves to remain unmindful of the state of Europe, which the conquests of the French Revolution and Empire had utterly deranged. The Pope was restored to his temporal sovereignty; Italy and Germany were brought back, with a few trifling exceptions, to what they had been previous to the Revolution; Ferdinand, the son of Charles, resumed the throne of Spain; and Holland and Belgium, being united into one kingdom, were assigned to the house of [Orange] Nassau, the head of which became, thenceforth, King of the Netherlands [Belgium breaking away in 1830].

> Arrangements were likewise made for the promotion of a good understanding, and the encouragement of commerce and the arts of peace, in all lands. But of the effects of all this legislation no time was afforded to make trial, when an event befell, which, however it ought to have been foreseen and provided against, affected the whole civilised world with astonishment.

> From his lonely habitation on the isle of Elba, Napoleon Buonaparte still kept up a communication with the world; and

discovering, or being willing to believe, that the [restored kings of France the] Bourbons were unpopular, he resolved to become again an actor on the stage of politics. He suddenly quitted his retreat; and throwing himself into the heart of France, was joined, wherever he appeared, by the troops, who carried him back in triumph to the capital. The colonel who commanded the 7th regiment of the line, and whom his master especially trusted, was the first to assume the tri-coloured cockade, and to distribute it to his followers. In like manner Marshal Ney, after pledging himself to bring back the invader in chains, not only joined his standard, but brought over his whole army. Thus was Louis [XVIII] deserted, one after another, by all in whom he had reposed confidence, and driven once more to seek personal safety in flight from a kingdom which he had entered only a year ago amid the shouts and blessings of the populace.

When intelligence of Buonaparte's escape from Elba first reached Vienna, where the ministers of the allied sovereigns were met in congress to discuss the affairs of Europe, it excited shouts of laughter. In proportion as reports came in, however, descriptive of the absolute success of the enterprise, kings and ministers changed their tone. Europe again flew to arms; and a proclamation being puiblished, in which Buonaparte was declared to have placed himself out of the protection of law, Russia, Austria, Prussia, and Great Britain hastened to bring their armies into the field. The Duke of Wellington assembled his force, which consisted of 30,000 British, 8,000 of the German legion, and a large number of Hanoverians, Belgians, and others, on whom little reliance could be placed, so as to cover the great road that leads from Avesnes to Brussels. The Marshal Prince [Gerhard Leberecht von] Blucher [(1742–1819)], who commanded the Prussians, established himself in front of Namur; and the communication was kept up between the left of the one and the right of the other, by patrols. Such was their condition in the end of May, 1815; while the troops of the Northern Powers were rapidly organising themselves, and threatening the other frontier of France, to the amount of nearly 300,000 men. But Napoleon, who soon discovered that his peaceful overtures were not likely to be attended to, resolved to strike at the corps which held the Netherlands ere the allies could come up. With this view, he put himself at the head of one of the finest armies that ever followed leader; and announcing, with his usual brevity, 'I go to measure myself with Wellington', advanced by hasty strides upon Brussels.

The French army, though superior in point of numbers to either the Prussians or the English, taken separately, could not hope to act against them united, with success. Buonaparte, therefore, made his dispositions to overwhelm them in detail; and pouring his masses first upon Blucher, dislodged him on June 16, after a fierce encounter, from the position which he had taken up at Ligny. While that terrible struggle was going on, [Michel] Ney [(1769–1815)], at the head of 43,000 men, engaged the advance of the British at Quatre Bras, but could not, though far surpassing it in numbers, make any impression. On the following day, however, Wellington, made aware of the overthrow of Blucher, fell back to the position of Waterloo, the soldiers marching under a heavy rain, and continually exposed, in the rear, to attacks from the French cavalry. That night, officers and men bivouacked behind the ridge on which they were to contend for life or death on the morrow, while Napoleon, leaving General Emmanuel Grouchy [(1766–1847)] with a corps of 30,000 men to watch the Prussians, hastened with the remainder of his force to occupy another ridge, about long cannon-shot distance. Both sides looked anxiously for the dawn, which came in, as the darkness had closed around them, with heavy showers and frequent gusts of wind. Still no movement was made by the enemy: indeed it was eleven o'clock before their rear was well closed up, and the arrangements of their leader were complete. But, in about half an hour afterwards, just as the last of the storm wore itself out, a fierce cannonade opened from the French guns, and columns of horse and foot pressed gallantly up the slope.

A country house which stood on the right flank of the British line, and a farm house on the left centre, were repeatedly attacked, and the latter carried, after a murderous resistance. On swept the cuirassiers like an iron cataract, through the interval thus opened;

and firm stood the squares of British infantry to receive them. Nor were the English cavalry, particularly the heavy brigade, idle. They charged the choicest of the French horse, overthrew them with great slaughter, drove their horses against the flanks of columns of infantry, and sabred large numbers, till the whole of the field was covered with the bodies of the dead and dying, whom in the confusion of the strife their very comrades trampled under foot.

In this manner the battle raged from noon tilll six o'clock in the evening, every attempt on the part of the French to penetrate the English line being defeated; while the English, gradually moving on as each successive wave was rolled back, found themselves thrown into a new order, with their flanks considerably advanced. It was then that Buonaparte, whom a few straggling shots on his flank warned of the approach through the wood of the indefatigable Blucher, resolved to make his last effort. All that could be collected, both of horse and foot, were formed into one dense column, and launched, amid loud cries of 'Vive l'Empereur!' against the British centre. The head of that column crossed the ridge, but never came within push of bayonet with the English, who stood in ranks four deep to receive them, for there fell such a storm of fire on its front, and both its flanks, and the heavy brigade charged so home upon the men as they staggered, that an attempt to deploy brought with it irretrievable confusion, and all order, all discipline, was lost. Then there was seen a spectacle such as a British army can alone display, when Wellington, waving his hat, gave the word for the line to advance. Down went man and horse on the side of the French, while a wild cry arising, 'Let them save themselves who can', the rout became universal.

Wearied with their exertions throughout the day, the English left to the Prussians, who had now come up, the care of following the fugitives; and well and willingly was that duty discharged. Little quarter was given by men whose bosoms burned with the recollections of a thousand wrongs which those nearest and dearest to them had suffered; so that all the roads, for many miles beyond the field, were covered with slaughtered men. Meanwhile Buonaparte himself galloped back to Paris, where the utmost dimay prevailed. He spoke of raising fresh levies, but was answered with questions as to the state of the army which he had led to slaughter, till finding that his hour had come, he again abdicated, and thought only of providing for his own personal safety. He fled to the coast, and having rthere surrendered to Captain Maitland [(1777–1839)], who commanded the 'Bellerophon', an English ship of war, he was by him conveyed, as a sort of state prisoner, to Plymouth. He was not permitted to plant a foot on the English shore; but being transported to St Helena, a rocky island in the middle of the southern Atlantic, he there, though surrounded with all the comforts which were consistent with a due regard to his safe keeping, dragged out some years of misery. Disappointed ambition – it may be remorse for the crimes of other days – soured his temper, and preyed upon his vitals; and he died at last on 5 May 1821, of a disease to which his family was liable – a cancer of the stomach.

The battle of Waterloo put an end at once to the hostile disposition of the French people...

I

Painting Waterloo

George Orwell, while still a prep-schoolboy named Eric Blair (1903–1950), smouldered with resentment against the school's proud display of a 'steel engraving of the charge of the Scots Greys at Waterloo, all looking as if they enjoyed every moment of it'. His posthumously published essay 'Such, Such were the Joys' complained that 'we were supposed to admire the Scots because they were "grim" and "dour" ("stern" was perhaps the key word) and irresistible on the field of battle'.

The most likely possibility is that the picture was not a steel engraving but a cheap copy of a very well-known painting, or if actually an engraving then one intended to recall its famous original, *Scotland Forever!* painted in 1881 by Elizabeth Lady Butler (1846–1933). In fairness to Butler, her soldiers do not noticeably radiate enjoyment: they look as if they are expecting to be killed, and while galloping towards Death and Glory are not obsessionally suicidal. The real-life originals in 1815 were not galloping, the ground making it too perilous: heavy dragoons, they were trotting. 279 out of 300 men and 16 out of 24 officers were killed. Forty years after, they were remembered as comparable to that generation's Crimean War massacre, the charge of the Light Brigade at Balaclava in 1854, immortalised by Alfred Tennyson (1809–92) in his lines:

> Half a league, half a league,
> Half a league onward,
> All in the Valley of Death
> Rode the six hundred.

But that was grossly unjust to the officers and men at Waterloo. Their action in the circumstances made perfectly good sense, if the battle itself made sense. The fate of the Light Brigade at Balaclava arose from an atrocious blunder.

Lady Butler was English, not Scots, but if the adult Orwell was aware of her he might have known she was something he disliked even more than the Scots: a convert to Roman Catholicism. In 1877 she had married the future Lieutenant-General Sir William Butler (1838–1910) GCB, PC, an Irish Catholic from birth. Orwell recalled the picture as symbolic of 'Our picture of Scotland... made up of burns, braes, kilts, sporrans, claymores, bagpipes and the line, all somehow mixed up with the invigorating effects of porridge, Protestantism and a cold climate', but that pillar of Protestantism Queen Victoria (1819–1901, rgd from 1483) had no problem with the Butlers' Popery. After his service in the battle of Tel-el-Kabir in 1882, William Butler was appointed her aide, and she had already commissioned Elizabeth Butler's *The Defence of Rorke's Drift* (1880). The painter was by now famous for her depictions of inspirational military moments of UK history, and in fact caught the imagination of the country as well as that of the Queen amidst the grim reports of the Second Afghan War when she produced the horrifying picture of a half-dead Dr William Brydon (1811–73) on horseback half-fainting within sight of Jalabalad in 1842 after the First Afghan War disaster which had wiped out virtually all the troops among whom he had served: it was entitled *Remnants of an Army*. It was certainly this painting the young Arthur Conan Doyle had in mind when creating Sherlock Holmes in *A Study in Scarlet* (1887), which begins with Dr Watson's horseback rescue from death in the 1879 Battle of Maiwand. Originally Conan Doyle had toyed with opening the story in the First Afghan War rather than the Second, and certainly Brydon is one of the more obvious sources of Watson.

Elizabeth Butler riveted the eyes of her audience on the wounded Brydon symbolic in his own wounded body of the slaughter whence he had fled, but even she could hardly show the worst effect, the loss of part of his skull. Nevertheless he served again before settling in Rossshire in 1859. His brother-in-law Major-General Donald Macintyre VC (1831–1903), served in the

Second Afghan War and was known to the Queen as recipient of her Victoria Cross the most esteemed honour she could bestow. Macintyre was Scots, Brydon was of Scots descent, and Victoria, now deeply under the influence of her devoted servant and possible morganatic husband John Brown, was infatuated with Scotland. So *Scotland Forever!* looks like the result of a very firm suggestion in theme and title from Elizabeth Butler's patron, Victoria. Its fame still flourished as long as the centenary of Waterloo, 1915, although by then somewhat eclipsed by the Armageddon raging in Europe, and Eric Blair, still at prep school, continued to smoulder his detestation of it. It was deeply implicated in his sense of Scotland as a hunting-ground, shooting-range, fishing-stockyard for the wealthy parents of his more snobbish schoolfellows. Its memory was still painful 30 years after, when he was writing or revising his prose ode on an insufficiently distant prospect of his prep school before entering the obvious extension of its values Eton. But by then he was losing his Scotophobia while living in the Scottish island of Jura, a haven in the dark world inspiring his *Nineteen Eighty-Four* (1949).

Scotland Forever! may have been Elizabeth Butler's artistic discovery of the UK's northern country in all its military glory, but the persuasive patron could point to her successful previous foray in 1875: 'The 28th Regiment at Quatre Bras' evoking the prelude battle to Waterloo where the islanders held back French assaults under Marshal Michel Ney, but whose intensity prevented their rescuing their Prussian allies from defeat at Ligny. The three battles were still remembered together, satirised by the Francophile Hilaire Belloc, who in his *Cautionary Tales for Children* (1908) had a father reprove his son (scared by his first sight of the newly-invented motor-car) with the shame of his inadequacy by heroic family standards:

> What would your Great Grandfather who
> Was Aide-de-Camp to General Brue,
> And lost a leg at Waterloo,
> And Quatre-Bras and Ligny too! ...

Belloc's illustrator, Lord Basil Blackwood (1870–1917) rose magnificently to the triple occasion with three similar but diminishing miniatures of the gallant ancestor losing the same leg alongside the name of each battle. He himself would be killed serving in the UK forces during the Great War. But the 28th Regiment were Gloucestershires. The title for the Butler Scottish Waterloo painting was sufficiently obvious for Victoria to have suggested it, being the war-cry of the Scots Greys (otherwise the 2nd Regiment), several of whom in her *Scotland Forever!* were apparently roaring it as their horses hurtled against the troops of Napoleon suggesting defiance rather than the elation morosely ascribed to them by the future George Orwell. In any case Butler was characterised by her ability to convey varying emotions and responses on the faces of the multitude of soldiers she brought to life in military drama. The title was famous enough to be used as a punch-like in one of the earliest *Biggles* magazine stories set in World War 1 and written by the air combat veteran W. E. Johns (1893–1968) in 1933, where his hero Biggles having been rescued by Scottish troops from capture by the Germans hails his rescuers with the punch-line *Scotland Forever!* which would also be the story title chosen to woo potential readers (reprinted in *Biggles of the Camel Squadron* (1934)).

Victoria could also have pointed to the Waterloo precedents in Scottish art, notably by Sir David Wilkie (1785–1841) and Sir William Allan (1782–1850) both knighted by herself and successively her Royal Limner in Scotland. Such enjoyment as their work had given her would be recalled by memories of her late husband, the glorified Prince Albert (1819–1861) with whom she had discovered Scotland. Both Scottish artists had had their most famous Waterloo paintings bought by the national hero of the battle, Arthur Wellesley (1769–1852) first Duke of Wellington. Wilkie was commissioned a year or so after Waterloo by Wellington to paint 'a parcel of old soldiers' relaxing outside an inn. That his concern was to honour the common soldiers in realistic terms deserves emphasis.

A hard-bitten Irish Protestant, Wellington had a generic necessity to despise sentimentality, which left to itself might encourage the lower orders (Catholic or otherwise) to become greater security risks than they already were. His bluntness made more mysteries than might be supposed: the famous reply (never fully authenticated) when called an Irishman – 'if a man is born in a stable, does that make him a horse?' – becomes more ironic when spoken in his neighing voice. And presumably he knew that he sounded like that. If he said it, it squelched the subject under discussion, whatever he intended, and Wellington certainly knew that to permit attention to his Irishness was to increase his vulnerability in an offensively status-obsessed metropolis, determined to despise Irish, Welsh, and Scots peripheries. Walter Scott, perpetually asserting the identities of all three, wrote 'For A' That an' A' That (A New Song to an Old Tune)' in 1814 – a light-hearted variation on the famous eponymous salutation to humanity by Robert Burns (1759–96) – in which his premature rejoicings on the fall of Napoleon included the restoration of the French Royalist fleur-de-lis:

> We'll twine her in a friendly knot
> With England's rose, and a' that;
> The shamrock shall not be forgot,
> For Wellington made braw that.

And Wellington was Scott's great hero among the living, a hero who came to like Scott's conversation and attention.

He was not the only intrusion on Burns's verse from the era of Waterloo. Napoleon was made to do duty for Robert Bruce's opponent King Edward. Philip J. Haythornthwaite's *Waterloo Men* (1999) reprinted the version of Burns's Bruce's Address supposedly sung as the Scots approached Bannockburn and recorded by Lieutenant James Hope of the 92nd as altered when the Comte d'Erlon attacked:

> Now's the day and now's the hour
> See the front of battle lour

See approach Napoleon's power
Chains and slavery!
Lay the proud usurper low
Tyrants fall in every foe
Liberty's in every blow
Let us do or die!

Whoever imposed Napoleon on the existing verse must have known the original version well, and have frequently sung it – so Napoleon was prompting Scots' identification with the UK cause. Scottish nationalism was really sinking itself in Hiberno-British at Waterloo.

We owe it to Wellington to respect his regard for soldiers when he showed it. He commissioned the painting of old soldiers from Wilkie at the end of a visit to his studio where he walked around and evidently liked Wilkie's talent for showing contrasts and kinship among individuals in a conventional scene. An inn in the King's Road, Chelsea, was suggested, and Wilkie wondered about a theme or story to give motive to the picture. Wellington thought the old soldiers might be playing skittles, clearly an appropriate accompaniment for beer. Posterity too easily remembered his calling his troops 'an Infamous Army' when preparing for Waterloo (when he was being starved of soldiers by the London civil service). He sufficiently identified with his men to think of their likes and dislikes with a sardonic pride. He accepted Wilkie's idea that one of them might be reading a newspaper. And Wilkie then painted *Chelsea Pensioners Reading the Gazette of the Battle of Waterloo*. It took him six years to finish, he charged Wellington £2,600, and when it was exhibited barriers had to be set up outside the Royal Academy for the first time in its history as thousands clamoured to view it. Professor Linda Colley's *Britons: the Forging of the Nation 1707–1837* (1992) saw Wilkie's use of a Welsh horse soldier's stretch towards the *Gazette*, a black military bandsman's reach to read it, Irish Scots and English ex-soldiers and civilian men and women, as affirmation of war having been 'the making of Great Britain'. She was right, but should have said 'the United Kingdom' which now embraced the entire archipelago including the birthplace of Wellington. And the picture above all was a celebration of peace after war. The magic of the name 'Waterloo' was the ending of international conflict after a quarter-century, culminating in victory, even if it pitched the economy into the doldrums.

The popular historian Christopher Hibbert (1924–2008) linked *Chelsea Pensioners* to the generous Wellington's payment of the same sum for Sir William Allan's *The Battle of Waterloo from the English Side* (1843). It is a long, brooding landscape darkened by great clouds in the sky with diminished humans and ominous artillery, lacking Wilkie's imagination or Butler's individualities. On arrival to collect his fee, Allan was startled to be paid in 'laboriously' counted notes, and suggested:

'Your Grace might prefer to draw a cheque on your bank to save time and trouble.'

'Do you suppose', the Duke replied, continuing to count the notes, 'I am going to let Coutts's people know what a damned fool I've been?'

[Hibbert, *Wellington – a Personal History* (1997), 204–5 and n.]

2

Soldiers

Rudyard Kipling is credited with giving the UK common soldier a voice. At least he forced his readers to realise that common soldiers had voices, something previously conceded grudgingly if at all. Kipling may have captured some reality, and imposed himself and his not always predictable prejudices at other points. But he was not the first recorder or interpreter. Xenophon (c. 430–354 BC) may have given some voices from his 10,000 Greeks struggling their way out of a hostile Persian empire in 399 BC. Jean Froissart (c. 1337–1405) certainly does make us hear soldiers' voices, notably in bitter Scottish complaint about the greed of their unwelcome French allies landing in Scotland during the Hundred Years' War.

The Napoleonic wars brought the old soldier into much more formidable literary assertion, in some cases possibly even without adulteration by patrons, archivists or publishers. Arthur Conan Doyle's Brigadier Gerard stories in the 1890s and 1900s drew on French veterans' memoirs, often well worth revival in their own right. Earlier in the 19th century Ireland produced soldier' narratives notably through the lens of Charles Lever (1806–71), *Charles O'Malley the Irish Dragoon* (1841) reviving Waterloo, and using Scott's wise fool and judicious eccentric in the shape of Irish peasant servants whose value as entertainers enabled them to exploit their English comrades into performing Irish servants' duties while the Irish sang. The classic case was Mickey Free in *Charles O'Malley*:

> I'm sick of this marchin'
> Pipe courtin' and starchin'
> How nate we must be
> To be killt by the French.

I'm sick of paradin',
Through wet an' cowld wadin',
Or standin' all night
To be shot in a thrench.
To the tune of a fife
They dispose of your life,
Or surrender your sowl
To an elegant lilt.
Now, I like Garryowen
When I hear it at home,
But it's not half so sweet
When you're goin' to be killt.

Walter Scott could make convincing soldiers with authentic voices and being the father of officers knew how to use their varieties of professionalism from the astrologer Guy Mannering in his eponymous novel (1815) to the pompous Gaelic-speaking Hector in *The Antiquary* (1816). But his great achievement was his realisation of the destruction of Gaelic Scotland as symbolised in the events of *Waverley*, and that theme resurfaced all too realistically in later works. 'The Highland Widow' (1827) claimed by him as very close to an original source lights up the tortured implications comic-tragic of recruitment of young Highlanders from Jacobite families and the sudden twists demanded by honour in the midst of destruction. It ties so directly with Kipling's 'Danny Deever' (1890) in *Barrack-Room Ballads* as to give formidable suspicion that it directly inspired it, turning as it does on murder and execution for a crime committed against a comrade. That in its turn leads to Oscar Wilde's (1854–1900) *Ballad of Reading Gaol* (1898), and it must have used his youthful memories of *The Highland Widow* also. (Wilde's son Vyvyan (1886–1967) recorded that his father used to sing a Gaelic song as lullaby to himself and his brothers, and Scott's 'My Aunt Margaret's Mirror' first published at the same date as 'The Highland Widow' (1827–28) quotes a Scots-Gaelic couplet of the same song.) The murder of a beloved comrade and friend is more directly confronted in Scott than elsewhere. Wilde's *Ballad* is openly based on a real soldier hanged for murdering his wife, and 'Danny Deever' is all the more effective for leaving motivation uncertain but it builds impressively on Scott's showing how the murderer's fellow-soldiers support his judgment and execution because they too loved the man he killed, and then are sent adrift in emotional reactions at the execution of what is, after all, their second comrade to die. In the all three cases the murderer has been taught to kill, and murder is his most natural way of confronting the loss of his honour. Scott was virtually saying that the destruction of Highland society through clearances, forfeitures, migrations, executions gave army recruitment as a way out but one in which killing could easily be the norm even when the enemy is not at hand.

Scott as the father of social history dug deeper into the social origins of recruitment than subsequent historians, partly because it needed the skills of both historian and novelist. We get little of that from surviving narrative by Scottish soldiers but we must turn to Scott for the background to Waterloo in human as well as in topographical and poetic terms.

The Scottish soldiers' narratives were forceful enough. Dr Jenni Daiches Calder in *The Story of the Scottish Soldier, 1600–1914* (1987) noted 6,070 Scottish officers and men of Scottish regiments taking part in Waterloo and its tributaries: 'The 71st regiment (1st Highland Light infantry) marched a day and a half without food and almost without pause to be in time for the battle... Bombarded by artillery and attacked by French cavalry they were then to suffer heavy losses.' Scots regiments suffered 436 killed and 200 wounded, some mortally. She singled out the highest point in the charge of the Royal Scots Greys when Sergeant (later Ensign) Ewart captured that Standard of the French 45th Regiment. Haythornthwaite quoted him in *Waterloo Men* (p. 56):

> ... The Enemy... and I had a contest for it; he thrust for my groin
> – I parried it off, and cut him through the head, after which I was
> attacked by one of their lancers who threw his lance at me, but
> missed the mark, by my throwing it off with my sword by my right

side; then I cut him from the chin upwards, which cut went
through his teeth; next I was attacked by a foot soldier, who, after
firing at me, charged me with his bayonet – but he very soon lost
the combat, for I parried it and cut him down through the head; so
that finished the contest for the Eagle. After which I presumed to
follow my comrades, Eagle and all, but was stopped by the General,
saying to me, 'You brave fellow, take that to the rear; you have
done enough until you get quit of it', which I was obliged to do, but
with great reluctance. I retired to a height, and stood there for
upwards of an hour...

Edinburgh Castle still preserves the Standard and the sword.
Edinburgh still has a pub on the Lawnmarket, near the Castle,
named the Ensign Ewart. Of course it also has an insalubrious
establishment named Burke and Hare's. But William Burke (1792–
1829), not yet a Scotsman, never got to Waterloo, although
Wellington requested that the Irish militia in which Burke was
serving and which Wellington had founded should be despatched
in time for the battle. But the London civil service rejected his
application. The regulations stated that the militia could only
serve in time of war, and Britain was not at war during the battle
of Waterloo. Napoleon was now not a government official
anywhere, not even Elba where he had been confined in 1814
before breaking out, so the action was purely a police affair being
simply to arrest a private person. One wonders what Ensign
Ewart and his fellows would have thought if they ever learned it.
What Wellington said about it on receiving the information may
be fairly readily surmised.

a   The Paisleyite from Edinburgh

Private Thomas Howell of the 71st Highlanders did not need to
be Scottish. His autobiography begins with his insisting his name
is not his own, that he was brought up in Edinburgh with devoted
but puritanical parents from whom he parted having appalled them
by seeking a career in the theatre where he failed. His assurance
of the falseness of his identity is strengthened by his version of his

youth and departure appearing theatrical enough in themselves to discourage any belief in their veracity. They sound more Welsh than Scottish, but many a good Scot has begun under different national colours. There may be some significance in his choice of the name of a Welsh king, the good Hywel Dda (c. 880–950) of Deheuberth, south-west Wales. His identification of his birthplace in Edinburgh sounds unreal. His origin may have been Highland though even that could be false. The friendless beginning is inconsistent with the nostalgic and more clannish end. Yet the military content of his memoirs has a true ring and his Scotticisms seem natural enough. It may be that the dubious Edinburgh origin was a disguise for Paisley, whose improbability is challenged in the last passage included here.

Be that as it might, *Journal of a Soldier of the 71st, or Glasgow Regiment, Highland Light Infantry, from 1806 to 1815 including particulars of the Battles of Vimeira, Lorunna, Vittoria, the Pyrennees, Toulouse, and Waterloo* went in to at least four editions from 1819 to 1828, and won an introduction by Christopher Hibbert in 1975.

The 71st had seen plenty of action under Wellington in the Peninsular War and losses were indiscriminately made up. Its men were sent to Ireland after Napoleon's abdication in 1814 and on his subsequent return to France the 71st soon found themselves near Brussels whence they were told to intercept the army from France (not to be confused with the French army):

We immediately marched off towards the French frontier. We had a very severe march of 16 miles, expecting to halt and be quartered in every town through which we passed. We knew not where we were marching. About one o'clock in the morning we were halted in a village. A brigade of Brunswickers marching out, we took their quarters, hungry and weary.

Next morning, the 17th, we got our allowance of liquor and moved on until the heat of the day when we encamped, and and our baggage was ordered to take the high road to Brussels. We sent out fatigue parties for water, and set a-cooking. Our fires were not well kindled when we got orders to fall in and move on along the high road towards Waterloo. The whole length of the road was very much crowded by artillery and ammunition carts, all advancing towards Waterloo. The troops were much embarrassed in marching, the roads were so crowded. As soon as we arrived on the ground, we formed in column. The rain began to pour. The firing had never ceased all yesterday and to day, at a distance. We encamped and began to cook, when the enemy came in sight and again spoiled our cooking. We advanced towards them. When we reached the height they retired; which caused the whole army to get under arms and move to their positions. Night coming on, we stood under arms for some time. The army then retired to their own rear and lay down under arms, leaving the 71st to advance. During the whole night the rain never ceased. Two hours after daybreak General [Sir Rowland] Hill [(1772–1842)] came down, taking away the left sub-division of the 10th Company to cover his recognisance. Shortly afterwards we got half an allowance of liquor, which was the most welcome thing I ever received. I was so stiff and sore from the rain I could not move with freedom for some time. A little afterwards, the weather clearing up, we began to clean our arms and prepare for action. The whole of the opposite heights were covered by the enemy.

A young lad who had joined but a short time before, said to me, while we were cleaning: 'Tom, you are an old soldier, and have escaped often, and have every chance to escape this time also. I am sure I am to fall.' – 'Nonsense, be not gloomy.' – 'I am certain', he said: 'All I ask is that you were tell my parents, when you get home, that I ask God's pardon for the evil I have done and the grief I have given them. Be sure to tell I died praying for their blessing and pardon.' I grew dull myself, but gave him all the heart I could. He only shook his head: I could say nothing to alter his belief.

The artillery had been tearing away, since day-break, in different parts of the line. About twelve o'clock we received orders to fall in for attack. We then marched up to our position, where we lay on the face of a brae, covering a brigade of guns. We were so overcome by the fatigue of the two days' march that, scarce had we lain down, until many of us fell asleep. I slept sound, for some time, while the cannon-balls plunging in amongst us, killed a great many. I was suddenly awakened. A ball struck the ground a little below me, turned me heels-over-head, broke my musket in pieces, and killed a lad by my side. I was stunned and confused, and knew not whether I was wounded or not. I felt a numbness in my arm for sometime.

We lay thus, about an hour and a half, under a dreadful fire, which cost us about 60 men, while we had never fired a shot. The balls were falling thick amongst us. The young man I lately spoke of lost his legs by a shot at this time. They were cut very close: he soon bled to death. 'Tom', he said, 'remember your charge: my mother wept sore when my brother died in her arms. Do not tell her all how I died; if she saw me thus, it would break her heart: farewell, God bless my parents!' He said no more, his lips quivered and he ceased to breathe.

About two o'clock, a squadron of lancers came down, hurraying, to charge the brigade of guns: they knew not what was in the rear. General [Sir Edward] Barnes [(1776–1838)] gave the word, 'Form square'. In a moment the whole brigade were on their feet, ready to receive the enemy. The General said, 'Seventy-first, I have often heard of your bravery, I hope it will not be worse than it has been today.' Down they came upon our square. We soon put them to the right-about.

Shortly after we received orders to move to the heights. Onwards we marched, and stood, for a short time, in square; receiving cavalry every now and then. The noise and smoke were dreadful. At this time I could see but a very little way from me, but all around the wounded and slain lay very thick. We then moved on in column, for a considerable way, and formed line; gave three cheers, fired a few volleys, charged the enemy, and drove them back.

At this moment a squadron of cavalry rode furiously down upon our line. Scarce had we time to form. The square was only complete in front when they were upon the points of our bayonets. Many of our men were out of place. There was a good deal of jostling, for a minute or two, and a good deal of laughing. Our quarter-master lost his bonnet, in riding into the square; got it up, put it on, back foremost, and wore it thus all day. Not a moment had we to regard our dress. A French General lay dead in the square; he had a number of ornaments upon his breast. Our men fell to plucking them off, pushing each other as they passed, and snatching at them.

We stood in square, for some time, whilst the 13th dragoons and a squadron of French dragoons were engaged. The 13th dragoons retiring to the rear of our column, we gave the French a volley, which put them to the right-about; then the 13th at them again. They did this, for some time; we cheering the 13th, and feeling every blow they received. When a Frenchman fell, we shouted; and when one of the 13th, we groaned. We wished to join them, but were forced to stand in square.

The whole army retired to the heights in the rear; the French closely pursuing to our formation, where we stood, four deep, for a considerable time. As we fell back, a shot cut the straps of the knapsack of one near me; it fell, and was rolling away. He snatched it up, saying, 'I am not to lose you that way, you are all I have left in the world'; tied it on the best manner he could and marched on.

Lord Wellington came riding up. [He had been Duke for a year, but a veteran of the Peninsular war naturally thought of him by the name by which he was known then.] We formed square, with him in our centre, to receive cavalry. Shortly the whole army received orders to advance. We moved forwards in two columns, four deep, the French retiring at the same time. We were charged several times in our advance. This was our last effort; nothing could impede us. The whole of the enemy retired, leaving their guns and ammunition and every other thing behind. We moved on towards a village, and charged right through, killing great numbers, the village was so crowded. We then formed on the other side of it and lay down under the canopy of heaven, hungry and wearied to death. We had been oppressed, all day, by the weight of our blankets and great coats, which were drenched with rain, and lay upon our shoulders like logs of wood.

Scarce was my body stretched upon the ground when sleep closed my eyes. Next morning, when I awoke, I was quite stupid. The whole night, my mind had been harassed by dreams. I was fighting and charging, re-acting the scenes of the day, which were strangely jumbled with the scenes I had been in before. I rose up and looked around, and began to recollect. The events of the 18th came before me, one by one; still they were confused, the whole appearing as an unpleasant dream. My comrades began to awake and talk of it; then the events were embodied as realities. Many an action had I been in, wherein the individual exertions of our regiment had been much greater, and our fighting more severe; but never had I been where the firing was so dreadful, and the noise so great. When I looked over the field of battle, it was covered and heaped in many places; figures moving up and down upon it. The wounded crawling along the rows of the dead, was a horrible spectacle: yet I looked on with less concern, I must say, at the moment, than I have felt at an accident, when in quarters. I have been sad at the burial of a comrade who died of sickness in the hospital, and followed him almost in tears; yet have I seen, after a battle, 50 men put into the same trench, and comrades amongst them, almost with indifference. I looked over the field of Waterloo as a matter of course – a matter of small concern. In the morning we got half an allowance of liquor; and remained here until mid-day, under arms; then received orders to cook. When cooking was over, we marched on towards France. Nothing particular happened before reaching Paris, where we lay in the lines until the French capitulated. We had our posts planted at each side of the city. The French troops retired; and we got under arms and marched towards the gates. We had a cannon on each side of the gate, and gunners, with lighted matches, standing by them. We marched into the city; passed Lord Wellington, who stood at the gates, and were encamped on the main road in the Thuilleries, where we remained all the time we were here.

In marching through the city, a lad, dressed as a Frenchman, was looking up the companies very anxiously. One of our men said, 'Knock the French fellow down'. 'Dinna be sae fast, man', said he: we stared to hear broad Scotch in Paris at this time. 'I am looking for my cousin', he added, naming him; but he had been left behind, wounded.

When we were in camp before the Thuilleries, the first day, two girls were looking very eagerly up and down the regiment, when we were on parade. 'Do you mind a careless husband, my dear', said one of our lads. – 'May be; will you be't?' said a Glasgow voice. 'Where the devil do you come from?' said the rough fellow. 'We're Paisley lasses, this is our regiment: we want to see if there's ony body here we ken.' The soldier, who was a Glasgow lad, could not speak. There is a music in our native tongue, in a foreign land, where it is not to be looked for, that often melts the heart when we hear it unexpectedly. Those two girls had found their way from Paisley to Paris, and were working at tambouring, and did very well.

It is not great literature. The provenance of its author seems beyond all discovery. Yet his perception and vision at moments seem Tolstoyan.

b   The Dunkeld Sergeant and the Lochaber Colonel

If 'Howell' deliberately left his personal hinterland a mystery, Sergeant D. Robertson never clears up the identity of his first name, perhaps through no fault of his own. We have no reason to suspect him of mendacity such as 'Howell' invites. He brought out his *Journal of Sergeant D. Robertson, late 92d Foot, comprising the different campaigns, between the years 1797 and 1818, in Egypt, Walcheren, Denmark, Sweden, Portugal, Spain, France, and Belgium* in September 1842 from Dunkeld whence his regiment's historian Colonel C. Greenhill Gardyne (a name which certainly might have been suspected of creation from an Edinburgh address) called him 'Duncan' but A.J. Henderson, bringing out the second edition of the *Journal* in 1981, cited the relevant documents in

London's Public Record Office to prove his name was 'David'. When a non-commissioned officer's memoir manages to breast the ocean of reminiscences by officers, it takes 140 years to determine his full name. A.J. Henderson warmed his readers' hearts by giving particulars from documents which established his discharge on 22 June 1818 when he was 41, 5 feet 9 inches tall, of fair hair and complexion, grey-eyed and a shoemaker 'by trade' (said Henderson) 'to trade' (Robertson might have said). He had enlisted in the Caithness Highlanders in 1795 when he would have been 17 or 18 although in his published *Journal* he misremembered that as 1797. This was most likely a natural error, but his silence on his own background might indicate one reason for enlistment, to cover up some offence detected or otherwise, criminal or political (not categories easily distinguished when workingmen came under suspicion in those days).

Some Robertsons were highly respectable, notably the Reverend William Robertson (1721–93) founder of modern scientific historiography in the English language (which he seldom spoke), best-selling historian of Scotland, Europe, and Latin America, Principal of Edinburgh University, firmly and remuneratively Hanoverian in allegiance. But other Robertsons had other loyalties. The chief of the clan Robertson published poetry in English rather than Gaelic and had been Jacobite in 1689, 1715, and 1745. Our David (not Duncan) began his *Journal* as published in 1842:

> Being brought up in troublous times, and the war arising out of the French Revolution fast approaching, I became fond of a military life; and, in the year 1797, at which period the disturbances in the north country arose about the balloting of the militia, I entered a company of volunteers which the Duke of Atholl had obtained permission to raise; but after being some time in it, I found the life not such as I was led to expect – there was not enough of bustle and variety in it for me; and the same changeless routine of duty, and scene of the Grampians, induced me to leave the corps, which I did, and entered into the Caithness Highlanders, then commanded by Sir John Sinclair [(1754–1835)],

and in which I had not been many days enlisted, when I was
ordered to Ireland along with the regiment.

A.J. Henderson is faintly uneasy about this, chiefly because the
records uncovered by him put Robertson's entry into the
Caithness Highlanders on 5 April 1795, transferring to the 92nd
Foot on 7 July 1800, while his service towards a pension began in
1798. Possibly the most frequent error made by autobiographers
is to imagine their long-ago careers took place in different dates
than what they did, or that their events happened in a different
order. There is little reason to believe that Robertson was covering
anything up, apart from the fact that he is covering virtually
everything up. The Athol Dukes had been highly respectable
from the third Duke (1729–74) who sold the Isle of Man to the
Treasury in 1765 and been given the Scottish premier order of
knighthood, the Thistle, in 1767, again a case of profitable
Hanoverian allegiance. However, his father, Lord George Murray
(1694–1760) had been an unhappy Jacobite general in the 1745
uprising and had died an outlaw, after which his son claimed the
Dukedom of Athol in 1764 having married the daughter of his
uncle the second Duke. Jacobites were history now, but the
traditions of divided loyalties were vigorous. The attractions of
alienated politics might still be to France, but a revolutionary
France, beckoning after 1789, however faintly. If so, it was not a
matter to be written about lightly, if at all. And what Robertson
does tell his readers is that he had little education, while his
literacy rather than non-literacy is conspicuous; the literacy might
have led him into teenage radicalism, however superficial,
necessitating judicious immersion among loyal soldiery. In
particular the elision of the mid-1790s may be relevant, and so
too is his retrospective political agnosticism on Ireland. 'It was
immediately at the close of the rebellion in that unhappy country
when we arrived there, and we had little or no duty to perform.'
Even for enlistment as late as 1797 Ireland was hardly passive
what with the attempted French invasion of 1796, the ferocious
military repression of 1797, the insurrections raging up and down

the east coast in 1798. As it is, Robertson's preface certainly does reveal military ambitions from the earliest youth he is ready to talk about, and his boyhood dreams may not have been as specific in their allegiance as they later became. If his formal text opens abruptly, his preface begins beguilingly but revealingly on the limits of an education which now as he commences his literary activity means more to him than ever, and those limits in 1795 might also have been responsible for bringing a frown to the brow of authority and a judicious enlistment:

> The Author of the following pages considers it necessary to lay before the public, ere they enter upon a perusal of his work, a few of his reasons for presenting them with a narrative of his life and transactions throughout the whole period of the late French War, during which time he was more or less an actor in that continued scene of blood and strife, of hardship and suffering, from the opening of his military career on the burning plains of Egypt, till the close of the drama on the triumphant field of Waterloo.

> In the Author's youth, it was not common for those of his station in life to receive so liberal an education as is now the custom, when 'the schoolmaster is abroad' which tended greatly to circumscribe his means and opportunities of deriving mental advantage from the scenes and circumstance which afterward surrounded him in the course of his wanderings having entered the army while very young, and being immediately hurried to the field of action, he had not the opportunity now afforded to young men in commencing their military life by the establishment of Regimental Schools, which, the Author hopes, will be the means of raising the British army to that height of mental improvement in the estimation of the philanthropist, which it presents to the military man of glory and renown.

He goes on to speak of literary friends who read his first draft, of the one who died while reading it, among whose effects his heirs lost it, of its recovery and of more fruitful friends of wide contemporary literary knowledge:

> They said that it was not uncommon to meet with works
> purporting to be soldiers' journals, in the pages of which war was
> described in all its 'pomp and circumstance', accompanied with
> all the beauties of language which gratify a literary taste; yet they
> afford to the reader no idea of the hardships and miseries
> experienced by those who constitute the ranks of an army, nor of
> the terrible desolation which it occasions in the country that has
> the misfortune to be doomed to bear its dreadful visitation. Those
> who take their notions of a soldier's life from the perusal of such
> writings, form but a poor estimate of the privations and sufferings
> which the British army endured in the different campaigns in
> which the Author bore an active part.

It would be easy to conclude from this nominally 'plain and intelligible language' that our narrative has been edited as the author originally hoped would be done by the friend who inconveniently and improvidently died. No doubt it is a more mature work than a draft soon after discharge would have proved. But while excessively insistent on the simplicity of his language, he is obviously fond of Shakespeare (1564–1616) and reads him as a military man would, which merits acceptance: in fact, to say it is too educated to be genuine, is to make the same case that today is foolishly made against Shakespeare's having written Shakespeare. Many people, some illustrious, have used the words 'pomp and circumstance' but very few have done so with the soldier's precision it requires. It is normally isolated from its context, which is in fact the successful general Othello suddenly seeing his world crashing before him as he is led to believe in his wife's infidelity, and he mourns most of all what had given him his utmost pleasure outside of marriage:

> Farewell the plumed troop and the big wars
> That make ambition virtue! O, farewell!
> Farewell the neighing steed and the shrill trump,
> The spirit-stirring drum, the ear-piercing fife,
> The royal banner, and all quality,
> Pride, pomp and circumstance of glorious war!

That is a soldier's close reading of the text. We have another instance of it on the eve of Waterloo just after the opening of his Chapter VII:

> On the 26th January, 1815, we marched to Cork again, with the intention of embarking for Scotland; but, owing to certain circumstances, we were detained until the 1st of May, when, instead of embarking for our native country, we were ordered off to Belgium again to take up our quarters in the tented field, 'grim-visaged war' having once more put on his 'wrinkled front', and was already shaking the continent with his fiery thunders.

Once again the sergeant is reading his Shakespeare with a soldier's eye. The quotation here is from the speech beginning *The Tragedy of King Richard the Third*, in which Richard, still only King Edward IV's brother the Duke of Gloucester, is meditating satirically on the prettification of court politics:

> Grim-visag'd war hath smooth'd his wrinkl'd front;
> And now, instead of mounting barbed steeds,
> To fright the souls of fearful adversaries, –
> He capers nimbly in a lady's chamber
> To the lascivious pleasing of a lute.

Since Richard is to blossom rapidly as a stage villain (essentially Punch as George Bernard Shaw (1856–1950) pointed out when reviewing the play), readers or viewers normally think of the passage as prologue. But the sergeant has clearer eyes than us. To him Richard (1452–85, rgd from 1483) is what he actually was, and that is a soldier, brave, resourceful, ambitious, and ready to die game. In fact he reminds us of the obvious motive for Shakespeare's Richard however otherwise unhistorical the portrait, that to a natural soldier intrigue and even treachery are symptoms of a professional, resenting removal from his sphere of success. With it comes a most interesting identification of Napoleon with Shakespeare's Richard not to speak of the Congress of Vienna in 1814 as the court of Edward IV at peace, a peace in itself an overwhelming temptation to a great soldier. It is not complimentary to Richard or to Napoleon: for a soldier to see his potential enemies as the Spirit of War does not means he likes either them or that Spirit. But he knows them for what they are and why. To resume our sergeant's tale:

> After getting safely on board, we weighed anchor on the 3rd, and on the 8th, landed at Ostend, and disembarked next day. We halted here, and got three days' rations served out, which we managed to get cooked. In the evening we embarked on board the boats on the canal, and proceeded to Ghent, where we arrived on the 11th at daybreak.

> It happened to be the weekly market-day when we landed, and none of us ever saw such a sight before. The day was beautiful, and the people were coming in boats from all directions to the centre of the city, which caused great stir and bustle; and to add to the effect of the scene, we were disembarked at the large market-place. If the novelty of what we saw made an impression on our minds, the Belgians were no less surprised at our strange appearance, as, I believe, none of them had ever seen any clad in the Highland garb before.

> We were all regularly billeted upon the inhabitants without distinction, and were civilly used by them. In a few days we were joined by our brethren and countrymen in arms – the Royal Scots, 42nd, and 79th, and a happier junction could not have taken place than that of meeting with so many Scotchmen, and more especially those brave fellows with whom we had fought side by side in Egypt and Denmark – at Corruna, Fontes, and Vittoria – among the Pyrenees – at Bayonne and Toulouse; and that we had met once more, 'Brothers in arms, but rivals in renown', ready to do battle for the honour of our common country. None but those who have experienced the fatigues, privations, and danger of war, can appreciate the worth of a veteran in arms. Only think of thousands of men meeting together, without perhaps knowing one another, but banded together by the feeling that they are fighting in the same cause, each individual doing his best to sustain the ancient reputation of his country – a reputation gained

by his ancestors in many a hard-fought battle. Among soldiers, the participation of the same sufferings and dangers creates and cements a friendship which can be but faintly conceived by those who were never exposed to the same perils. We were all highly overjoyed at meeting again, little knowing that ere long we would be called upon to engage in a battle which would unite us more closely in friendship than ever.

All very well, but to what country does this allude? The UK? Britain? Scotland? Here the quotation unlocks the code. 'Brothers in arms, but rivals in renown' is a line in Scott's 'The Landing of the British Army in Portugal' (the landing being on 1 August 1808, effectively beginning the future Wellington's Peninsular military career). The poem itself was in fact a popular extrapolation from Scott's late entry in his series of epics begun magnificently and professionally with *The Lay of the Last Minstrel* (1805) and 'Marmion' (1808), *The Vision of Don Roderick* (1811) in which the (real) last Gothic king of Spain ultimately killed in the Moors' successful invasion in 714 BC supposedly sees a succession of future visions culminating in the Peninsular War in which Wellington's advent hailed the heterogeneity of the British army (verses LVIII–LX):

> A various host – from kindred realms they come,
> Brothers in arms, but rivals in renown, –
> From yon fair bands shall merry England claim,
> And with their deeds of valours deck her crown.

In other words, England will claim what successes may befall, and it is interesting to see that complaint loud and powerful 200 years ago. But Scott bestows his chiefest blessing on his actual fellow-countrymen:

> And O! loved warriors of the Minstrel's land!
> Yonder your bonnets nod, your tartans wave!
> The rugged form may mark the mountain band
> And harsher features, and a mien more grave.
> But ne'er in battle-field throbb'd heart so brave

As that which beats beneath the Scottish plaid,
And when the pibroch bids the battle rave,
And level for the charge your arms are laid,
Where lives the desperate foe, that for such onset stayed.

The Sergeant happily quoting the popular phrase coined by the Scottish Whig lawyer and future Lord Chancellor Henry Brougham (1778–1868) speaking in 1825 to London working men 'the schoolmaster abroad' was probably excessively optimistic in assuming his readers of all classes – above all the Scottish lower classes – would automatically identify his quotations, although those we have noted were from two very popular Shakespeare plays and soldiers who liked ringing verse might be expected to know Scott's 'The Landing of the British Army in Portugal', in readily available anthology (*The Flower Vase*) as early as 1823. We had better be humble about our superiority in historical knowledge to his contemporary observation – he knew a lot more about what early 19th-century soldiers read than we do. He clearly took their recognition of his quotations' literary and political contexts. This poem by Scott bore a very clear message: England might egotistically absorb, unquestioning, the achievements of the Scots as well as her own, but the Scots, while perhaps cruder, harsher, uglier, were a vital British necessity. And not only the Scots. The third verse extolled the Irish, united to Britain in Parliament as well as in King since 1801:

Boast, Erin, boast them! Tameless, frank and free
Rough Nature's children, humorous as she.
And HE, yon chieftain – strike the proudest tone
Of thy bold harp, green Isle! – the Hero is thine own.

This was proclaiming equality under the Union with a vengeance even if the Sergeant must readily have known it for equality as cannon-fodder, skilfully deploying the beguilements of a recruiting sergeant. It preaches the same lesson anent Ireland as Scotland: a reliable army depends on popular and command acceptance of ethnic equality. It was nationalist, albeit nationalist in the cause of Union. But the great father of Irish constitutionalist nationalism, Daniel O'Connell, holding his mass support in hand by demand of Repeal of the Union, nevertheless declaimed in the 1830s that treatment of Ireland on the same level of equality as England would make Repeal unnecessary. And Scott, self-acknowledged pupil of the deep social novelist Maria Edgeworth (1767–1849) and friend of the popular songmaker Thomas Moore (1779–1852), could draw notes as true from the Irish harp as from the Scottish pipes. To make a virtue for British arms from the notorious Irish rebelliousness in the happily contrived 'tameless' was remarkable indeed. On inspection it was the same argument he made with the Scots, celebrating the heroism of Jacobites without reservation as essential for contemporary British interests. His choice of Irish qualities were if anything more apposite than the virtues of the recently pacified Highlanders whom he forced his fellow-Lowlanders to accept not simply as equals but even as national symbols into which in 1822 he poured the gross weight of George IV (1762–1830 Regent from 1811, rgd from 1820). And Wellington, with or without a stable, is triumphantly deified as Irish. As the Sergeant acknowledged, this was the stuff to give the troops.

And English predominance was made the means of claiming not only military virtues but also radical doctrines in patriotic service. 'The Landing of the British army in Portugal' used its first line to grasp the nettle of military invasion signalling the advent of oppression (verses LVI, LVIII):

It was a dread, yet spirit-stirring sight!

And he was quick to claim the English – and hence the British and Irish when comrades in arms – 'bold in Freedom's cause' holding 'the scorn of death in Freedom's cause':

the blunt speech that bursts without a pause
And freeborn thoughts which league the Soldier with the Laws.

Classical as well as modern history could give too many examples of horrors created by invading armies given license by their generals. Scott's ideal British army was to be regarded as treating laws as master of armies, friend of civilians. We resume the Sergeant's narrative conscious that he, through Scott, unites the diverse dates and lands of Wellington's command into a meaningful totality for his soldiers:

We remained in Ghent till the 28th of the month, without the occurrence of any thing worthy of notice, when we marched to Brussels, where the Duke of Wellington had his head-quarters, and were put in divisions under the command of Sir Thomas Picton [(1758–1815)], Sir James Kempt, [(1764–1854)], and Sir Denis Pack [(c. 1772–1823)]. When we came to Alast, half way between Ghent and Brussels, we found [Charles Ferdinand (1778–1820) second son of the future Charles X (1757–1836 reigned 1824–30)] the Duc de Berri commanding a body of French troops that adhered to the Bourbon cause. Almost all the officers had served in the French [Napoleonic] army in Spain, and some of them had been in Egypt. The latter, upon seeing the Highland regiments, immediately came running to meet us; and asked very kindly 'If they had not seen us before?' When we answered in the affirmative, they went and told the Duke, who expressed his happiness to have such supporters to aid the cause of his house.

On our arrival at Brussels we were billeted throughout the city. The 28th, 32nd, 34th, 95th, and two battalions of the Hanoverian militia, joined us here, which were paraded in brigade every second day. While here we had a grand review, which was attended by all the resident Belgian and English nobility. Recruiting for the Belgian army was going on with great activity, and hundreds daily marching to the different depots. They were mostly all good-looking young fellows, and had a very soldier-like appearance. We were now served with four days' bread, and supplied with camp-kettles, bill-hooks, and every thing necessary for a campaign, which, according to all accounts, was fast approaching. The inhabitants, like those of Ghent, were very civil and kind to us, and we, in turn, were the same to them. We were kept in a state of alarm for some days, from reports that appeared in the Belgian papers to the effect that the French troops were moving on to the frontiers.

('Belgium', Austrian for the previous century, had now been awarded to the Netherlands whose ruler William took the title 'King of the Netherlands' on 16 March 1815. Belgium revolted successfully in 1830 and became independent. But 'Belgium' and 'Belgian' were widely used in 1815, not merely in retrospect from after 1830.

> In order to avoid being taken at unawares, the orderly sergeants were desired to take a list of the men's quarters, with the names of the streets, and the numbers of the houses. It was also arranged that every company and regiment should be billeted in the same, or the adjacent streets, to prevent confusion if called out at a moment's warning.

> On the evening of the 15th of June, the sergeants on duty were all in the orderly room till ten o'clock at night; and no orders having been issued, we went home to our quarters. I had newly lain down in bed when the bugle sounded the alarm, the drums beat to arms, bagpipes played, and all was in commotion – thus stunning the drowsy ear of night [Byron, Childe Harold's Pilgrimage, Canto I (1812), Stanza 2] by all kinds of martial music sounding in every street. Upon hearing this, sergeants and corporals ran to the quarters of their respective parties to turn them out. I went to the quarter-master for bread, and four days' allowance was given out of the store, which was soon distributed among the men – every one getting his share and speedily falling into rank. So regular and orderly was the affair gone about, that we were ready to march in half an hour after the first sound of the bugle. Colonel Cameron [(1771–1815)] had that day been invested with the Order of the Bath, by the title of Sir John Cameron of Fassifern, and was present at a splendid ball, given by the Duke of Wellington in the park, when the alarm was sounded. [Here the text in MacKenzie MacBride (ed.), With Napoleon at Waterloo (1911) is adulterated by silent editorial interpolation largely accurately if inauthentically inserting before 'the Duke of Wellington' '[[Lady Charlotte] the Duchess of Richmond [(1768–1842)] daughter of the seventh [correctly 'Alexander fourth'] Duke of Gordon [(1743–1827)] who was brother to the Marquis of Huntly [wrong]. She had invited

some sergeants of the 92nd to show the company especially the Belgians, the Highland reel and sword dance, which they did.' [deleting 'in the park'. The Duchess's husband was Charles Lennox (1764–1819), fourth Duke of Richmond and Lennox and their son Charles Gordon-Lennox (1791–1860), fifth Duke of Richmond and Lennox, was assistant military secretary to Wellington in Portugal (1810–14). That the sergeant ascribed the hosting of the ball to Wellington is a likeable indication of his priorities. In any case the permission to hold the ball came from Wellington.] He was quickly at our head; and we commenced our march at daybreak, leaving the city by the Namour gate, followed by the inhabitants, to whom we gave three farewell cheers, and they returned very sorrowful, thinking that many of us would never return. [Last 13 words deleted silently in MacKenzie MacBride.}

As it is impossible for any soldier, who is immediately engaged with his own company in the field of action, and whose range of observation must consequently be very limited, to give a detailed description of a battle in which he took a part, I will endeavour to narrate as correctly as possible what came under my own notice – thus avoiding an error into which many writers on this subject have fallen, by making statements chiefly from hearsay and upon the authority of others, which are not substantiated by facts and supported by ocular demonstration. I shall, therefore, try to steer clear as much as possible of this fault, and give the reader such an account of this decisive engagement as will bear the strictest scrutiny. [Paragraph deleted in MacKenzie MacBride.]

When we had got a few miles from Brussels we entered a wood, the trees of which were remarkably tall; and although the road was very wide it was wet and soft, as the sun did not strike upon it to make it dry. During our march we had several times to diverge to the right and left, to avoid the bad parts of the road. When we had got a good way into the wood, we met a number of wagons conveying Prussian soldiers who had been wounded the day before, who told us that the French were driving all before them, and that we were greatly needed. As we are ['were' in MacKenzie MacBride] too apt to entertain bad opinions, we suspected treachery on the part of the foreigners, and that we should have to retreat; for we did not credit much what the Prussians told us of the affair.

We continued our route until we came to the skirt of the wood, into which we were marched, and ordered to lie down and rest ourselves for two hours, but not to kindle any fires, and on no account to move out of our places. We lay down and slept for some time, when the Duke of Wellington and his staff rode by, which made us move, but we were not called upon to march. While lying here we were joined by a great many Hanoverians and Brunswickers, all of whom were formed up in the wood. When we emerged into open ground, we found ourselves at the village of Waterloo. About eleven o'clock we fell in, and marched on. The day was oppressively warm, and the road very dusty. We moved on slowly till we reached the village of Geneppe, where the inhabitants had large tubs filled with water standing at the doors, ready for us, of which we stood in great need. They told us that a French patrol had been there that morning. We had hardly got out of the town when we heard the sound of cannon at no great distance, which proceeded from the place where the conflict was going on between the French and the Belgians. The sound had a stimulating effect upon us; for so eager were we to enter the field of action, that we felt as fresh as if we had newly started. In fact, we were all anxious to assist the poor Belgians, who were but young soldiers, and consequently but little experienced in military affairs. 'Forward' was now the word that ran through all the ranks; but the Colonel had more discretion, and would not allow us to run, lest we should exhaust ourselves before the time. He issued peremptory orders that every man should keep his rank as if on parade, and not to march above three miles an hour. The firing seemed to be coming nearer as we approached a farm and public-house, called Quatre-Bras.

We now went off the road to the left of the house, and closed up upon the front division, in columns of battalions ready to form line. Before many minutes had elapsed, we received some shots from the French artillery which galled us considerably, as we had none up yet to return the compliment. The French made a movement to their own right; and the 42nd and 79th were ordered to oppose them, in a field on which was growing a crop of long wheat or rye. As those regiments were moving on to take possession of a wood to the left, a little in front of our position, they were attacked by a strong body of cavalry, which made considerable havoc among them. The 92nd was now brought to the front of the farm-house, and formed on the road, with our backs to the walls of the building and garden, our right resting upon the cross-roads, and our left extending down the front. We were ordered to prime and load, and sit down with our firelocks in our hands, at the same time keeping in line. The ground we occupied rose with a slight elevation, and was directly in front of the road along which the French were advancing.

Shortly after we had formed here, the Duke of Wellington and his staff came and dismounted in rear of the centre of our regiment, and ordered the grenadier company to wheel back on the left, and the light company on the right; so that the walls of the house and garden in our rear, with the eight companies in front, joined in a square, in case that any of the enemy's cavalry should attack us. We had not been long in this way, when a column of Brunswick hussars, with the Duke of Brunswick at their head, made a charge down the road on the right. In this, however, they were unsuccessful, and were driven back with considerable loss, the Duke being among the slain.

(Friedrich Wilhelm (1771–1815) Duke of Brunswick, brother-in-law of the future George IV, had defended and briefly retaken his Duchy's capital from Napoleon and having been put to flight by him in 1809 was lieutenant-general in the UK army., with his personal troops the 'Black Brunswickers' taken into UK pay. His mother Augusta (1737–1813) was the elder sister of George III (1738–1820, rgd from 1760).

The column of French cavalry that drove back the Brunswickers retired a little, then reformed, and prepared to charge our regiment; but we took it more coolly than the Brunswickers did.

When the Duke of Wellington saw them approach, he ordered our left wing to fire to the right, and the right wing to fire to the left, by which we crossed the fire; and a man and horse affording such a large object for an aim, very few of them escaped. The horses were brought down, and the riders, if not killed, were made prisoners. Some of them had the audacity to draw their swords upon the men when in the act of taking them, but such temerity only served to accelerate their own destruction; for in the infuriated state of mind in which we were at the moment, those guilty of such conduct fared a worse fate than those who submitted without a murmur.

We were informed by the prisoners that Napoleon himself was in the field, as were our old friends, [Nicolas Jean de Dieu] Soult [(1769–1851)] and Ney; and that Ney was directly in our front, and had ordered the charge to be made upon us. We were very happy on hearing this intelligence, as the thought that the two great generals of the time were to meet each other on the field of battle, stimulated us to do our utmost to maintain unsullied the hard-earned reputation which the British army had gained in many a bloody battle field. As far as I am aware, this was the first time that ever the Emperor had been personally engaged with us, and we were anxious to know if the same good fortune which attended his former campaigns still awaited him, and whether he would be able to re-enact the splendid achievements of Ledi, Marengo, and Austerlitz, when brought into the arena of action against an army for the most part composed of veteran troops, and commanded by brave and experienced generals. We wished to show him that we were made of sterner stuff than those whom he was wont to chase over the length and breadth of Europe, and that though all the Continent should again fall under his iron sway, yet there was one little isle of the sea that would brave his colossal strength, and defy him to his teeth. [Last 33 words omitted in MacKenzie MacBride.] But to return to our narrative.

Immediately after the enemy's cavalry had been driven back, and partially destroyed, a column of infantry was sent round to a wood on our right, and another to push us in front. At this time the 30th,

69th, and 73rd regiments joined us, upon which we left our ground to charge down the road, led by General [Edward] Barnes [(1776–1838)] and Colonel Cameron. Just as we had taken our stand, a volley was fired at the Duke of Wellington from behind a garden hedge. As I was the first sergeant he observed on turning round, he ordered me to take a section and drive them out. By the time I got out of the garden and came to the road, the regiment was closely engaged with the bayonet. The lieutenant-colonel at this time was coming up as fast as he could ride, having been shot through the groin. We immediately joined the regiment at the foot of the garden, and advanced at full speed, the French having by this time given way. In the impetuosity of our charge we had advanced too near the enemy's guns, and were obliged to move off to the right to the skirts of the wood. We then advanced rapidly on the right, and turned the left flank of the French.

We now made a determined attack to seize two of the enemy's guns, which gave us considerable annoyance, but were foiled in the attempt. At this time the Guards came up, and the action began to be general. We, however, still sustained considerable loss from the enemy's cannon, as we had none with which to oppose them; and as so few of our troops had come up, we could not form a sufficiently strong column in one place to enable us to take any of their artillery from them. Our regiment was now very much cut up in both officers and men, as we had been first in the action, and, along with the other Highland regiments, had for a long time to resist the attack of the whole French army. We continued very warmly engaged until about eight o'clock in the evening, when we rallied, and made another effort to capture some of the enemy's guns. In this attempt I received a wound in the head, while in the act of cheering the men forward. I was very sick for a short time, and was sent to the rear under the care of the surgeon, where I got my wound dressed, and remained till morning; and when I awoke I found I was able to join the regiment again. On account of this wound I was reported dead, and my old companions were rather surprised at my return. On calling over the roll the night previous, it was found that we had lost 1 colonel, 1 major, 4 captains, 2 lieutenants, 4 ensigns, 12 sergeants, and about 250 rank and file. ['12 lieutenants' in MacKenzie MacBride, obvious printer's error.]

The regiment was now formed in the rear of the house of Quatre-Bras. Before we had time to cook our victuals, the Duke of Wellington and his staff came into the midst of us, and gave orders for the march of the different divisions. The cavalry by this time were coming up in great strength; and on the arrival of General Hill at their head, we all stood up and gave him three hearty cheers, as we had long been under his command in the Peninsula, and loved him dearly, on account of his kind and fatherly conduct towards us. When he came among us he spoke in a very kindly manner, and inquired concerning our welfare. He also expressed his sorrow that the colonel was wounded; and gave us a high character to the Duke of Wellington, who replied that he knew what we could do, and that by-and-bye he would give us something to keep our hands in use. We now removed as many of the wounded out of the field as we could, and buried all the dead bodies within our reach, especially the officers.

After remaining here till about ten o'clock, we fell back to the skirts of a wood, near the village of Waterloo, the cavalry forming our rear guard. The French now pushed very hard upon us, but we still managed to keep the road. On coming to the village of Geneppe, the houses were full of our wounded, who had made that length, and were not able to go any farther. When the French came up they were all taken prisoners. We now heard that Colonel Cameron had died on the road, about an hour before we came to Geneppe.

Colonel Cameron's death was ultimately marked by a brief but elegantly quarto *Memoir of Colonel John Cameron, Fassiefern, KTS* (1858) by the Rev. Archibald Clerk (1813–1887) minister of Kilmallie, at the behest of Sir Duncan Cameron, Bart., of Fassiefern, for private circulation, with title-page epigraph mangled from Sir Walter Scott's 'The Dance of Death', timeously if not always felicitously penned in 1815 in honour of Highland aristocracy serving King George a half-century after their allegiance was still being sworn to King James and Prince Charlie. The full tribute it gave to Colonel Cameron ran:

Where, through battle's rout and reel,
Storm of shot and hedge of steel,
Let the grandson of Lochiel,
    Valient Fassiefern.
Through steel and shot he leads no more
Low laid, 'mid friends' and foemen's gore –
But long his native lake's wild shore,
And Sunart rough, and high Ardgower,
    And Morven long shall tell,
And proud Ben Nevis hear with awe
How upon bloody Quaker-Bras
Brave Cameron heard the mid hurra
    Of conquest as he fell.

Scott himself told John Bacon Sawrey Morritt (1771–1843) on 2 October 1815 that it had followed from his major poem 'The Field of Waterloo' and was 'an odd wild sort of thing'. Clerk wrote of John Cameron's death:

On the 13th he dined with the Duke of Wellington; and on the 15th he attended the celebrated ball given by the Duchess of Richmond, where 'Belgium's capital had gathered her beauty and her chivalry' [Byron, *Childe Harold's Pilgrimage* Canto III, Stanza 21, Line 2]. Late in the evening he was requested by the Duke to march with all speed to Quatre-Bras, and was, with characteristic caution, directed, as other officers were, to retire privately from the ball-room. He communicated with Mr Gordon, paymaster of the regiment, who had been, as formerly mentioned, for years on terms of the most cordial friendship with him, and on whose authority we state these minute details. They occupied the same billet. They walked together in it, and, familiar with danger, departed in the early morning without any anticipation of their being parted to meet no more.

Colonel Cameron marched forwards to Quatre Bras, animated and animating his men by the martial strains he loved so well. [Clerk then gave Byron's verse on the Cameron warpipes in 'The Eve of Waterloo', (*Childe Harold's Pilgrimage* Canto III, Stanza 26) still quoted with no attribution, whether because all readers were expected to know its origin or because Clerk felt that a Church of Scotland minister had best not write Byron's name.] By 2 p.m. he was in front of the enemy. The doings of that day are well known; but while the glory of Waterloo – 'the first and last of fields, king-making victory' [Byron again] – casts into the shade every other event of the 'hundred days', we doubt whether any day, until that of Inkermann [in the recent Crimean War] reflects brighter lustre on the stern Roman fortitude of the British, than does that of Quatre-Bras. With fearful odds against them, deserted by the Belgian horse, labouring under many sore and heavy disadvantages, they and the brave black Brunswickers, again and again repelled the French, led on by the fiery Ney – 'the bravest of the brave' –now more brave and fiery than ever, in order to cover with success the great treason of which he had been guilty. [Ney who had deserted Napoleon for the Bourbons had been sent by them to arrest him when he left Elba and entered France, but was unable to resist his old master's appeal, and joined him, and was executed for it after Waterloo by the restored Bourbons.] It was, however, at a terrible sacrifice that the British repulsed the French on that day. The noble 92nd was dreadfully thinned; many gallant officers, and about 300 privates, were struck down. But the loss which the survivors, which the army generally, as well as the great captain himself, regretted most deeply, was that of their Colonel, who here 'closed his life of fame by a death of glory'.

We give the account of his fall as related to us by an eye-witness still living to confirm the narrative. The regiment lined a ditch in front of the Namur road. The Duke of Wellington happened to be stationed among them. Colonel Cameron, seeing the French advance, asked permission to charge them. The Duke replied, 'Have patience, and you will have plenty of work by-and-by'. As they took possession of the farm-house, Cameron again asked leave to charge, and was again refused. At length, as they began to push on to the Charleroi road, the Duke exclaimed, 'Now, Cameron, is your time – take care of that road'. He instantly gave the spur to his horse; the regiment cleared the ditch at a bound, charged, and rapidly drove back the French; but while doing so, their leader was mortally wounded. A shot fired from the upper storey of the farm-house passed through his body, and his horse, pierced by several bullets, fell dead under him. His men raised a wild shout, rushed madly on the fated house, and, according to all accounts, inflicted dread vengeance on its doomed occupants.

Evan Macmillan [in childhood his foster-brother] who was ever near his master and friend, speedily gave such aid as he could. Carrying him, with the aid of another private, beyond reach of the firing, he procured a cart, whereon he laid him, carefully and tenderly propping his head on a breast than which they was none more faithful. The life-blood, however, was ebbing fast, and on reaching the village of Waterloo, where so many other brave hearts were soon after to bleed, Macmillan carried Fassiefern into a deserted house by the road side, and stretched him on the floor. He anxiously enquired how the day had gone, and how his beloved Highlanders had acquitted themselves. Hearing that, as usual, they had been victorious, he said, 'I die happy, and I trust my dear country will believe that I have served her faithfully'. His dying hour was soothed by that music which he had always loved, and which, while harsh and unmeaning to a stranger, is so intimately blended with a Highlander's deepest feelings, and most sacred memories, as to awaken his whole heart, to rouse up his whole being, and thus is highly esteemed in the hour of sorrow or of danger, in every great crisis of life. Better still his dying hour was soothed, and we trust blessed, by earnest prayer. And worthy of remark it is that these dying supplications were uttered in that mountain tongue – the first which he had heard in youth, and now, as we have known in kindred instances, at the close of life, naturally offering itself as the vehicle of the deepest aspirations of the soul in the most solemn of all situations.

Thus he met with a warrior's death, and more, with a Highland warrior's death. His remains were hastily interred in a green alley – Allee vert, on the Ghent road, under the terrific storm of the 17th, which, as has often been remarked, seemed to presage the

'dread confusion, noise, and garments rolled in blood' [Isaiah, ix.5]
that will render the 18th day ever memorable in the annals of
mankind. The funeral was attended, we need scarcely say, by the
attached McMillan, by Mr Gordon, already mentioned, and by a
few soldiers, disabled by the wounds of Quatre Bras from standing
aside their comrades in the fight, but still able and most willing to
pay this last tribute of respect and affection to their lamented
leader.

Thus the memoir compiled over 40 years later, but while showing
the different perspectives from the vantage-point of Colonel and
Sergeant, our picture of the dying Colonel is not from a class
superior to the Sergeant's – Clerk's source here is a private soldier,
Cameron's devoted Evan Macmillan, who lived on for some
decades. The text is clearly adulterated by Clerk's piety, and
possibly by Macmillan's alcohol which Clerk mentions: very little
articulacy is likely from dying men. But we can be confident in
the sound of the pipes, and Cameron's reversion to his first
language, Gaelic: that is attested in comparable linguistic cases.
For instance the Fenian Diarmuid O'Donovan Rossa (1831–
1915) drifted back into Gaelic in his last hours. Whether
Wellington's characteristic promise of more work by-and-bye
preceded Cameron's death or not may not be detectable, but the
probabilities lie with the version emanating from Evan Macmillan
who would probably have a harder grip on his beloved Cameron's
death, but exact chronology is more unreliable than detail of
incident. And now, back to the Sergeant, whose thoughts were
undoubtedly more with the fighting than with the dying:

We still kept moving very slowly, until the French artillery got up
close to our rear, and were annoying us very much, when the
Duke ordered a regiment of Hanoverian infantry to wait and assist
our cavalry, who were formed on each side of the road to protect
our flanks, and which they effectually did.

(Hanover was still part of King George's dominions and would
remain so until 1837 when its refusal to be ruled by a woman

prevented Victoria from inheriting it, and it passed to her next uncle in line, Ernest Augustus (1771–1851), Duke of Cumberland.)

We arrived at length at the house of Le Hay Saint, a very large building, having a great entrance gate on the left hand, where the Brussels road is cut through a small green hill, with high banks on each side. On coming to the rear of the house, we diverged to the right and left. The right of Sir Thomas Picton's division, to which we belonged, rested on the great road; and the left extended on in rear of a double hedge – that is two hedges with a bye-road running between them. It had been raining very hard ever since we commenced our march in the morning, and we were drenched to the skin. The ground on which we were formed had been lately ploughed, and the corn newly brairded, so that with the number of men treading upon it, the field was reduced to the consistency of mortar. However, we formed line; and the French halted opposite to us, much in the same state. The weather soon began to fair up, but still every thing below and around was very wet. We now thought of getting our muskets in order for action, for by every appearance we were likely to need them soon. I took the opportunity of going into the hedge to look at the French forming; but such numerous columns I had never looked on before, nor do I believe that any man in the British army had ever seen such a host. I must confess that, for my own part, when I saw them taking up their ground in such a regular manner, and every thing appearing so correct about all their movements, I could not help wishing that we had had more troops with which to oppose the thousands that were collecting in our front.

Our artillery and a rocket brigade had now arrived; all the cavalry had come up by this time; and a great number of foreign infantry had already joined us. The evening at length cleared up, but without any sunshine. We had a fine view of the country round the village of Mount St Jean, which stood within half a mile of our rear; and the skirts of the great forest of Soignes lay not much farther off. We could get no fuel here to make fires, as every thing was soaked with the rain. There was a field of green clover in our rear, of which we cut large quantities, and with some branches out of the hedges made a kind of bed on the ground to keep us from the clay. Every regiment sent to its own front a small piquet, for the purpose of giving information to the commanding officer in case of alarm. In this condition we stretched ourselves on uncomfortable lair. [From here to end of paragraph deleted in MacKenzie MacBride, rather oddly, given its value.] Every man's mind was engrossed by the thought that we were in the immediate neighbourhood of a powerful and hostile army, headed by a skilful and experienced leader, to whom that army was devotedly attached, and in whose cause every man in it was ready to peril his life. It might be said, in fact, that on our exertions the fate of Europe depended. In addition to this, there was not any apparent possibility of escape, if we should be discomfited, as the fields were quite open to cavalry as far as the forest, which was nearly a mile distant; while the ground being soft and heavy, and we were so encumbered and loaded with our wet blankets and clothes, that getting away seemed entirely out of the question. The contemplation of all these gloomy appearances threw a damp over our minds, but we tried to cheer our drooping spirits by the thought that we had never run out of the field; and the call began to pass from the one to the other what we should do after we had beaten the enemy.

In this state of mind we lay till about twelve o'clock, when the alarm was given that the French were coming. We instantly stood to our arms, and continued in that posture until the cause of the alarm was found to be groundless, which arose from a part of the Belgian cavalry going their rounds, and who, when challenged by our sentries, had replied in the French language. During all this time it continued to rain very hard. As we had lain down by fours, we had blankets enough to cover us and keep us dry; but when we got up again, we were made as wet as before. The place on which we lay was like a marsh, and, for the season of the year, the rain was very cold. Notwithstanding all these disagreeable circumstances, however, we lay down again, and slept sound, as we were very much fatigued.

We were aroused by daylight, on the morning of the 18th, and ordered to stand to our arms, till the line should be reconstructed. During the time I never felt colder in my life; every one of us was shaking like an aspen leaf. An allowance of gin was then served out to each of us, which had the effect of infusing warmth into our almost inanimate frames, as before we got it, we seemed as if under a fit of the ague. We remained on the ground till about six o'clock, when we were ordered to clean ourselves, dry our muskets, try to get forward, and commence cooking. We had scarcely got breakfast discussed, when a shot from the French killed one of our pioneers who was sleeping. We were now ordered to stand to our arms, plim and lord, fix bayonets, wheel into line, and be ready to act in any manner required. By this time the action had begun on the right, and the Duke and his staff had taken up their station on the green height in rear of Le Hay Saint, where he could see the whole of the line from right to left. Beyond the hedge in our front was a fallow field, having a gentle ascent towards it; and being placed rather in rear of the slope, the French cannoniers could not hit us with their shot, but they made some shells to bear upon us, which made great havoc in our ranks. As yet we had not fired a shot, but what had been discharged by our out-posts.

The French were now busy in forming columns to their own right, which was directly in our front, and we were expecting every moment to be attacked, as all on the right of our division were warmly engaged. We were well cautioned to be steady and keep together, as, in all likelihood, we would be first attacked by cavalry, who would try to break our line; and, above all, to mind what word of command was given – whether to form square, or whatever else the order might be. At this time, our men were falling fast from the grape shot and shells that the French were pouring in among us, while as yet we had not discharged a musket. The artillery attached to us had now commenced a brisk fire, which drew a great deal of the French fire upon our ranks, as we were immediately in rear of the artillery. At length a large column of French infantry was seen advancing in our direction. .

Every one was now eager to be led on, and as the way which they were taking indicated that it was upon that part of the line where the 92nd was stationed that the attack would be made, General Pack ordered us to advance, and line the hedge, to oppose the advance of the column. But when we got to the side of the hedge, we found the French were there as soon as we. We cheered loudly, and called to the Scotch Greys, who were formed up in our rear, 'Old Scotland for ever!' Upon which some person in the regiment called out to 'charge', when, all at once, the whole regiment broke through the hedge, and rushed headlong on the French column. The onset was so sudden and unexpected, that it threw them into confusion. At this critical moment, the Greys flew like a whirlwind to our assistance, and having got round on the flanks of the column, they placed themselves between the enemy and our own line. While we pushed them hard in front, the other cavalry regiments in the brigade, the Blues and Enniskillen Dragoons came at full speed to our aid, when it was fearful to see the carnage that took place. The dragoons were lopping off heads at every stroke, while the French were calling for quarter. We were also among them busy with the bayonet, and what the cavalry did not execute we completed; but, owing to the position taken up by the dragoons, very few of them escaped. It was here that some of the 92nd and the Greys had a struggle for the eagle, which a sergeant of the Greys bore off.

In this charge all the sergeants, and one of the officers at the colours, were killed. So terrible was the havoc which the Greys had made, and such the fearful impressions that they produced on the minds of the French, that nothing was heard from those among them that were literally trodden down, but to deliver them from those dragoons. A poor fellow cried out to me to save him, and he would give me his watch and all his money; but being called to the colours, I was obliged to leave him. One of our regiment, however, fortunately came to the place where he was, and as he spoke in good English, our fellow thought he was a Briton, and conducted him to the rear. We now returned to our old ground, as we could not retain possession of what we had acquired.

When we had resumed our old station, we found that we had lost a great many in the late affair, and among those that had fallen, was my particular and well-beloved comrade, Sergeant-Major Taylor. As I knew he had a valuable watch upon him, I went out between the fires of the two lines and took it, and some other tings, off him, for the behoof of his widow. We had not time yet to ascertain the amount of our loss, but I found that our captain had been wounded, and was amissing, and that I was left in command of two companies, as we lost all the subaltern officers on the 16th. On the right of our division, the French cavalry were making a dreadful push, and we often thought that they would force their way through our lines, but the firm and determined resistance of our troops at last convinced them that their efforts were unavailing.

After the charge already mentioned, we were not troubled for a long time, nor did we fire any for two hours. During all this time, however, we suffered much from the enemy's artillery. We were ordered to sit down and rest ourselves. During this intermission, we had a fine view of what was passing on the right. I could see the French cavalry make those terrible charges which frequently drove ours to the rear, but who, when they came to the forest, faced about, and beat them back in turn; and often, when the French cavalry were compelled to pull about, our infantry gave them a dreadful volley on the way when passing. It was, I suppose, at this stage of the action that the French account of the battle stated that they had possession of Mount St Jean; but, in truth, they did not keep it for one minute, as from where we were seated, I had a perfect sight of what was going forward. At this time, the 27th and 40th regiments had arrived from Brussels, and were forming column in front of the large farm house, on the outside of the village. Although the French cavalry had obtained possession of the village, it would have been impossible for them to have retained it, while our cavalry had the support of these regiments.

About four o'clock the enemy made another attack on our part of the line, by a large body of lancers, who rode up on our squares with as much coolness as if subjecting us to a regimental inspection. We kept up a smart fire upon them, however, and put them to the right-about. But before we had succeeded in turning them, they did us considerable damage by throwing their lances into our columns, which, being much longer than the firelock and bayonet, gave them a great advantage over us. At this time we could distinctly see large columns of infantry forming in our front, with numerous bodies of artillery, when we expected we were to be called upon to sustain a charge from all kinds of arms. We were again ordered to line our old hedge to be in readiness to receive them. When we saw the dense masses collecting in our front ready to rush upon us, we looked for nothing but that our line would be broken, and utter discomfiture would be the consequence. The bodies of our brave artillerymen lay beside the guns which they had so bravely managed, and many a cannon had not a gunner left to discharge it. At this time there was scarcely an officer left in our regiment, in consequence of which the command of the company devolved upon me. I now began to reflect on what should be done in case of a retreat becoming inevitable, over a long plain, in front of cavalry. I was aware it would be difficult for me to keep the men together, as they had never retreated before under similar circumstances. In fact, any word of command misunderstood in the smallest degree would be sure to produce disorder. And in the face of peril so imminent, there must always be some persons more afraid than others, whose timidity might infect the rest; whereas, when advancing to meet the enemy, every one becomes emboldened, and confusion is not as likely to occur.

While we were in this state, with life and death in the balance, the French column began to move forward. An awful pause ensued! Every man, however, was steady. At length they came within pistol-shot of our lines, when a volley of rockets was let off by a brigade that had been formed in the hedge, which threw them into entire confusion. To complete their disorder, we, at the same instant, gave a loud huzza, and poured a well-directed volley upon them. This unexpected and rather rough reception made them turn and run, leaving behind them a number of killed and wounded. When this brush was over, we sent out a few skirmishers in our front, along the hedge, merely to keep up the fire, and give information of what was happening among the French, who were still keeping up a distant cannonade. We now opened our files along the bridge, as the wider they were kept, there was less danger to be apprehended from the round shot, and in this way we remained for a long time. Notwithstanding this precaution, however, they were occasionally taking off some of us.

It was now seven o'clock, and by this time there was no officer in the regiment but the commanding officer (whose horse had been shot), the adjutant, and very few sergeants. I had charge of two companies, and was ordered to pay particular attention to any signal or movement I might see in front, for which purpose I was furnished with a spy-glass. In a short time one of our skirmishers came running in, and called to me to look at the French lines, as something extraordinary was going on. On the enemy's right I perceived that a cross fire had been commenced, and that troops in the same dress had turned the extremity of their line, and were advancing rapidly. I immediately informed the adjutant, who said that perhaps it was a mutiny in the French army, and that we would better form our companies close, so as to be ready to march to any point. At this instant, an aide-de-camp came galloping down our rear, and calling out, 'The day is ours – the Prussians have arrived'. All eyes were now turned to the right to look for the signal to charge, which was to be given by the Duke of Wellington. Never was reprieve more welcome to a death-doomed criminal. Nothing could stop our men, and it was only by force that the non-commissioned officers could keep them from dashing into the French lines. No language can express how the British army felt at this time; their joy was truly ecstatic.

By this time the aide-de-camp had returned to the Duke, who was standing in the stirrups with his hat elevated above his head. Every eye was fixed upon him, and all were waiting with impatience to make a finish of such a hard day's work. At last he gave three waves with his hat, and the loud three cheers that followed the signal were the heartiest that had been given that day. On seeing this, we leapt over the hedge that had been such a protection to us during the engagement, and in a few minutes we were among the French lines. Nothing was used now but the bayonet; for, after the volley we gave them, we set off at full speed, and did not take time to load. All was now destruction and confusion. The French at length ran off, throwing away knapsacks, firelocks, and every thing that was cumbersome, or that could impede their flight. One division at the farm house of La Belle Alliance made an attempt to stand, and came to the charge. When the three Highland regiments saw the resistance offered by this column, we rushed upon it like a legion of demons. Such was our excited and infuriated state of mind at the time, and being flushed with the thought of victory, we speedily put an end to their resistance. The Prussians were now among us – the one nation cheering on the other, while the bands were playing their national anthems.

It was now dark, and we were ordered to halt for the night, while the Prussians marched past us. The place where we were bivouacked was immediately at the end of the house where Bonaparte had stood all day which was by this time filled with the wounded. As we had not got any water during the day, numbers of us went in search of it. After looking about for some time, we at length discovered the draw-well, and accordingly supplied ourselves. The next morning I looked into the well, and discovered it was full of dead bodies; but as we were not aware of this circumstance when we drank the water, we never felt any bad effects from using it. In fact, we were not in a condition to quarrel about the quality of the liquid we got, as a cup of water of almost any kind was considered a boon by our unfortunate wounded comrades, who were suffering that insatiable and dreadful thirst which is experienced by men in their situation. The night was now far advanced; and as we could not see what was going on at a distance, we lay down to repose ourselves, cherishing the fond hope that as we had now vanquished the enemy, we would be permitted to sleep in peace. When morning came, I arose and went out to view the field, on which so many brave soldiers had perished. The scene which then met my eyes was horrible in the extreme. The number of the dead was far greater than I had ever seen on any former battle field. The bodies were not scattered over the ground, but were lying in heaps – men and horses mixed promiscuously together. It might truly have been called the 'crowning carnage' for death had indeed been here, and had left visible evidences of his grim presence in the misery and devastation that surrounded us. I turned away with disgust from this heart-melting spectacle, and had scarcely arrived at my quarters when every person that could be spared was sent out to carry the wounded to the road side, or any other convenient place where the wagons could be brought to convey them to hospital.

We had not proceeded far in this humane duty, when we were ordered to make ready, and at seven o'clock marched to the right to get on to the great road that leads to Paris. At any other time we would have hailed the order with joy, but a very different feeling now pervaded our minds. When we thought that we were called on to leave the place where so many of our brave companions were lying, without either seeing the dead interred or the wounded taken proper care of, our hearts were filled with grief and vexation. Numbers who had fought by our side on the preceding day were now stretched lifeless on an open field; and we were not permitted to give them the common rite of burial, and see them decently interred in the field where they had spent their heart's blood. I confess my feelings overcame me; I wept bitterly, and wished I had not been a witness of such a scene. And now the most harrowing part of the awful scene presented itself to our view. Being on the extreme left, we had to pass along between the two lines to the right. We moved on as silent as the dead that lay so thickly around us. No one could speak, so awestruck were we with the horrid spectacle. Here lay French and British in all the agonies of death, many of them calling on us to shoot them and put an end to their sufferings; while others were calling on us to come back, and not leave them exposed to the inclemency of the weather, to breathe their last in a land of strangers, with no friendly hand to comfort them and close their eyes in death.

The following is a list of the killed and wounded belonging to the 92nd, on the 16th and 18th days of June 1815, at Quatre Bras and Waterloo:

> June 16th, at Quatre Bras – 1 colonel, 2 captains, 1 lieutenant, 2 ensigns, 3 sergeants, and 61 rank and file. Total, 70.

> June 18th, at Waterloo – 1 major, 4 captains, 14 lieutenants, 4 ensigns, 1 surgeon, 10 sergeants, and 298 rank and file. Total, 332.

> Total of killed and wounded on both days, 402.

Having at last got on the great road to Paris, we had not marched many miles from the field when we took some prisoners, from whom we learned that Napoleon had set off for Paris. There was not an inhabitant to be seen, all having fled to the woods. We halted near a small village for the night, when the Duke of Wellington in person came up and thanked us for the manner in which we had conducted ourselves during the engagement, and lavished the highest eulogiums upon us for our exertions to uphold the reputation of the British army. But he had one fault to find with the 92nd, and that was for being so forward in crossing the hedge in the early part of the action. He said, as it turned out, all was well; but had it happened otherwise it might have ruined all his plans, and caused the destruction of the whole left wing of the army; and he urged us to pay attention to the words of command that might be issued next day. He then galloped off to pay his respects to the other regiments who had been similarly engaged.

On our march we went through Mons, passed Malplaquet, and went into the town of Catue, where Louis XVIII came up to us. Nothing worth mentioning happened until we came to St Dennis, a city within three leagues of Paris, where the French had collected a few guns, and commenced firing upon us from the works. We gave them a few rounds, and were preparing to carry the place by a *coup-de-main*, when the civil authorities hoisted the white flag, and we marched in, and filed off to the right bank of the Seine, while the other divisions took the left, and so on until we formed a complete circle round Paris. We halted, and got ready for a fresh action; but, by the time the line was formed, the garrison of Mont Martre displayed the white flag, which was soon seen flying from all the steeples of Paris. We immediately marched strong detachments to every barrier and entrance into the city. Every guard had two field-pieces, which were planted at the entrance of the streets, loaded, and the matches lighted and in readiness in case of any disturbance. These precautions, however, turned out to be unnecessary, as, with the exception of some very trifling demonstrations, the people exhibited no symptoms of rebellion. We were now ordered to get all our appointments and our clothing cleaned, and when that was done, we should have liberty to go into Paris by turns; and a hope was expressed that we would not quarrel with any of the French soldiers that might happen to be there.

It would be altogether superfluous for me to attempt to give any description of Paris after what has been said about it by many intelligent visitors, who were far better qualified to do so than I. Suffice it for me, then, to say, the city contains some very spacious and lofty edifices, and that the Seine is spanded by a number of elegant bridges. The polace of the Tuileries in a fine old building, with extensive gardens about it. The garden of plants and zoology has within its enclosurer a great collection of wild beasts, and other specimens of natural history.

After lying in Paris for some time, we were turned out to be reviewed by the crowned heads (but the French one was not there), and, among other manoeuvres, made a sham display of taking Mont Martre. Medals were now awarded us; but some disagreeable feeling was like to arise, when we heard that there was to be a difference in the material of which they were to be made. We were told that officers were to receive gold medals, while the privates' were to be composed of brass, which partiality nearly caused a mutiny. At length, when the Duke of Wellington learned the dissatisfaction that prevailed, he ordered that they should be all alike – that as we had shared equally in the dangers of the day, we should all partake alike of its glories. We remained in Paris till November, when we were shipped for England, and shortly after our arrival, were ordered for Scotland. On the road we were treated when great kindness, and entertained with hospitality in almost every place until we came to Edinburgh, from whence we marched to Ireland. I remained with my regiment here until 1818, when, owing to a disappointment in my promotion, and the increase of my family, I applied for my discharge, which, after some delay, was at last granted. Having got a pension for my services sufficient to support me, I finally wended my way to the place of my nativity, where I live in peace, far removed from those scenes of bloodshed and misery which it has been my lot to witness, and which I have thus attempted to describe.

And there Sergeant David Robertson left his readers in 1818, and after recovery and revision of his text, in 1842. The superiority of his text to the silently censored version from MacKenzie MacBride is obvious, but the deletions in the 1911 publication have some ironic implications. It shows a squeamishness indicating that reader from the Sergeant's generation and its immediate successor had stronger sensibilities than the later Victorians whose wars had been farther away. It indicates how unprepared the Edwardians were for the horrors to be unleashed on their doorsteps within a few years. It throws into clearer perspective the falsification of fighting conditions initially in World War 1, and the revulsion induced against lying propaganda and the whole war experience when the truth became known. The Sergeant also shows us the sharp, and occasionally even red-hot edges of class resentment, but his narrative is the more convincing because he seems deliberately to have avoided bitterness as much as possible. His horrific account of the failure to honour the dead and tend the wounded contrasts very significantly from Clerk's narrative of Colonel Cameron's corpse:

His father and friends resolved that his remains should not be left in a land of strangers, but should repose with those of his ancestors. Accordingly, in April of the following year, his youngest brother, accompanied by Macmillan, to identify the spot, opened the hastily-made grave of the Allee verte, and having secured the remains in a leaden coffin, brought them to Leith. His other brother, Sir Duncan, then in Edinburgh, applied for a King's ship to convey them to Lochaber. The request was readily granted, and after being kept for some days at Fassiefern, they were at length committed to their final resting-place in the churchyard of Kilmallie, within a ruinous aisle of the old church, where lie Sir Ewen Cameron of Lochiel, 'the Ulysses of the Highlands' [Macaulay's verdict in his *History of England* in which Lochiel is a minor if Jacobite hero] as well as many other Chiefs of the Clan. John of Fassiefern is also buried there, and their subsequently Sir Ewen of Fassiefern and Lady Cameron were laid. Sir Ewen at this time resided in Arthurstone, and from age and infirmity was unable to travel to Lochaber. The duty of chief mourner thus fell to Sir Duncan, who led a funeral procession such as Lochaber shall witness no more. He was accompanied by Lochiel, by Macneill of Barra, Macdonald of Glencoe, Campbell of Barcaldine, and many other gentlemen of the district, besides the relatives of the family; but still more, he was followed by three thousand Highlanders, who, with feelings responsive to the wailing notes of the lament poured forth from many bagpipes, sincerely mourned for the early death of one whose brave deeds were worthy of his high ancestry, and shed additional lustre on their country.

But even the gratifying homage to Cameron could not permanently stifle remaining class questions. Lord Archibald Campbell (1846–1913), son of the individualistic cabinet minister George (1823–1900) eighth Duke of Argyll, produced a very different story of Cameron's death in his *Records of Argyll* (1885) p. 90:

There is a story current in Dunstaffnage, which used to be told by an old pensioner who lived on the estate, and belonged to the district, that Colonel Cameron of Fassifern, of the 92nd, who was shot at Quatre-Bras, was shot by one of his own men, who was a bad character, and whom he had had flogged a few days before. The pensioner who told this had not got a very good name in the army himself; but he swore he knew it for a fact of his own knowledge, and also that the other man had told him that he was going to do it, and had done it. Both men are now dead.

There is this much to be said for the thesis, that Cameron was credited with an exceptionally foul mouth in rebuking his men. The habits of commanding officers were peculiarly horrific as instruments of punishment, inhuman sentences meted out for crimes like drunk on duty (300 lashes). The insult, degradation, and intolerable pain could well induce vows of vengeance. And a slaughterhouse like Waterloo was an admirable hiding-place for murder. We will never know the truth, but there was more to army service than heroic leaders and devoted followers. Whatever hidden traditions lingered among former soldiers on Cameron's death, the official version prevailed in inspirational literature a century later. The Reverend P. D. Thomson, Chaplain with the 1st and 4th Battalions in the field and Senior Chaplain of the Highland Division on the Rhine produced in December 1916 *The Gordon Highlanders, Being a Short History of the Services of the Regiment* 'by request' when on Service during the protracted horror of the Somme. The book continued 'an issue to all ranks throughout the remainder of the war' stated Colonel Commandant S. G. Craufurd, Black Watch and Gordon Brigade, Territorial Army in prefacing a new edition on Armistice Day 1920. The Chaplain, in the grimly unquestioning Christian militarism of World War 1, blended a vision of edifying savagery among the Highlanders with his own enlistment of God or appropriate equivalents:

In February 1815, Napoleon escaped from Elba, Europe was again plunged into war, and a British army, under Wellington, which included in its ranks the Gordon Highlanders, was despatched to the Continent. On the evening of 15th June, at the historic ball given in Brussels by the Duchess of Richmond, Wellington suddenly learnt that Napoleon had crossed the Belgian frontier at daybreak, and had sent Marshal Ney to engage the British, which he himself struck at the Prussians at Ligny. Wellington was ready. By daybreak on the 16th his army was en route for QUATRE-BRAS. Battle was joined in the forenoon, and raged all day. The 92nd in the 5th Division arrived on the scene at 2.30, and went into action immediately. Throughout the afternoon they sustained repeated charges of French infantry and cavalry. Wellington himself was an observer of the steady and effective way in which they met and broke charge after charge. At last, just before night-fall, their chance came. Immediately in front of them a French column, 1,200 to 1,500 strong, took post behind a house and garden. The word was given: and, led by their fiery and beloved chief, they leapt the ditch which they had been lining and charged home, performing prodigies of valour, but suffering heavily. Among others Cameron went down, struck by a bullet in the groin. His fall roused the Highlanders to a pitch of fury which nothing could withstand. They swept the French column before them; on other parts of the field the enemy gave way, fighting foot by foot; and by 9 o'clock victory was complete.

Next day, Wellington retired to WATERLOO, where the French and British armies faced each other on Sunday morning, 18th June, while Blucher with his defeated Prussians was at Wavre, some 18 miles away. The battle-field consisted roughly of two ridges with a valley between then, crossed by the high-road from Brussels to Charleroi. The 92nd, with the rest of the 5th Division under Picton, were posted just to the left of the road, immediately behind the ridge. Opposite them thundered French batteries to the number of 80 guns, under whose fire the French columns advanced across the valley to the attack. After a time the British troops in front were driven in, and Sir Denis Pack called upon the Gordon Highlanders to restore the situation – 'Ninety-Second, all the troops in front of you have given way; you must charge the column.' Just as they were about to charge, the Scots Greys came up, surging around both flanks of the Regiment and through lanes made for them by their kilted comrades. With shouts of 'Scotland forever!' both Regiments charged together, many of the Highlanders holding by the Greys' legs and stirrup-leathers as they swept forward in a wild and resistless rush. In three minutes the French column was completely shattered. His infantry having failed, Napoleon throughout the afternoon sent wave after wave of cavalry to capture the ridge; but, though fresh brigades were sent forward to smash the British by sheer weight, the solid squares stood firm, and all their efforts broke like waves upon the rocks. Finally, about 7 o'clock, he hurled his famous Guards in one crowning effort to break the stubborn line, only to see them thrown back like the rest. Just then the first corps of Blucher's army came up. Wellington, quick to see and seize the opportunity, held his cocked hat on high and waved it forward. The army advanced as it stood, the French were driven headlong, Waterloo was won, Napoleon's power was finally broken, and peace restored to the world. For their service in this brief but epoch-making campaign, the Gordon Highlanders bear on their colours the proud name of 'WATERLOO'.

This clerical packaging also made characteristic use of the notion of primeval Highlanders retaining enough primitive devotion to chiefs, vengeance, blood-worship, etc, to enhance their utility when civilisation needed to be set aside. The Lowlander and English image of the Highlanders could frighten itself comfortably by stress on such traits before Culloden, and rejoice after it that thanks to the Butcher Cumberland and similar agents of improvement the Highlanders were being tamed or at least controlled. The 1745 Jacobite rebellion had been part of the War of the Austrian Succession (1740–48), and during its sequel, the Seven Years' War (1756–63), Highlanders were being put to bloody work regardless of any attempt at prohibiting their rearmament. In Ireland penal laws against the recruitment of Catholics were being secretly avoided or ignored in the Seven Years' War and (more openly) during the War of American Independence (1775–1783). To draw the Highlanders into full cultural equality with all other forms of cannon-fodder necessitated the genius of Walter Scott (whose motives were civic rather than military but who knew heroic fame was the fastest road to mutual respect). By the time the Reverend P. D. Thomson endeavoured to draw in replacements for the slaughtered corpses at the Somme, the wild men had been transformed from frontier menaces to favoured Myrmidons.

c   The Last Survivor?

MacKenzie MacBride however real or pseudonymous was an Edwardian man of letters whether as historical novelist of early Anglo-Saxon England or song collector or topographer, who compiled *With Napoleon at Waterloo* in 1911. It included soldiers' narratives including substantial extracts from Sergeant Robertson's. It also included papers on Waterloo gathered together by an Edinburgh doctor of social consequence, Edward Bruce Low. We have to take his offerings, or their offerings, on trust, with the reminder that our experience of his handling of Sergeant Robertson's text warns us he serves up largely accurate but occasionally censored detail. And appropriately foremost among these texts are memories of the famous charge of the Scots Greys, well flagged up by its editors:

THE GREYS AT WATERLOO

REMINISCENCES OF THE LAST SURVIVOR OF THE FAMOUS CHARGE

The Greys at the glorious Waterloo fight
Put the thousand men of Count D'Erlon to flight,
Then eagle and banner by Ewart were won,
And the de'ils o' Dundee proved they're 'Second to None.'

Sergeant-Major [John] Dickson of the Scots Greys from whose lips many of the details of the battle of Waterloo here given were obtained by members of his family, was the last who survived of those who fought in the regiment at Waterloo. He was a native of Paisley, born in the Revolution year of 1789. He enlisted at Glasgow in 1807 when barely eighteen and remained in the service till 1834. At Waterloo he was corporal in Captain Vernon's troup, and his sabre and other regimentals bear evidence that his number was 57 of F troup. He was promoted sergeant after Waterloo for his services, and took the place of Sergeant Charles Ewart, who received a commission in the Fifth Veteran Regiment for the brave deed narrated here [capturing the enemy Standard].

On retiring from the Greys Sergeant Dickson joined the Fife Light Horse, and his long residence in Crail is fresh in the memory of many of the inhabitants. He died at the age of 90 on 16 July 1880, survived by three children and several grandchildren. His army papers bear witness that during his service of twenty-seven years in the Greys his character was 'excellent', and he was awarded a medal for long service and good conduct in addition to his Waterloo medal. He was a typical yeoman – tall, if ruddy complexion, brown hair, and hazel eyes, as the army record tells us – and his descendants still farm the acres in East Lothian which their ancestors have held from Lord Wemyss for generations.

Seated within the coffee-room of the little Fifeshire inn, a merry party of villagers and visitors met in the summer evening to do honour to their veteran host John Dickson, on the anniversary of Waterloo, in the year 1855. The news from the Crimea portended another attack upon Sebastapol, which in truth was taking place at that very moment; and as the thoughts of the people were with their kinsmen in the trenches, the genial host was induced to relate his experiences of 40 years ago.

Taking his 'yard of clay' pipe in hand, he seated himself at the table, at the head of which sat the village banker; for, be it known, 'Waterloo Day' was a high day in the village, kept in ripe memory by the flags flying and the procession of school children, decked in summer attire and gay with flowers, to do honour to 'mine host', whose deeds of valour were on every tongue. When the toddy-glasses had been filled it only required the key-note to be sounded by the inquiry of the president, 'By-the-bye, sergeant, what might you be doing just at this time forty years ago?' to draw forth the great story of the charge of the Union Brigade. The sergeant smoked for a time in silence; then, with a far-away look in his eyes, he began:

'Well, you all know that when I was a lad of eighteen, being a good Scotsman, I joined the Greys, the oldest regiment of dragoons in the British army, and our only Scottish cavalry corps.

'When news came that Napoleon Bonaparte had landed in France, we were sent across to Belgium post-haste, and there had a long rest, waiting for his next move. I remember how the trumpets roused us at four o'clock in the morning of Friday the 16th June 1815, and how quickly we assembled and fell in! 'Three days' biscuit were served out to us; and after long marches – for we did 50 miles that one day before we reached Quatre-Bras – we joined the rest of our brigade under [General] Sir William Ponsonby [(1772–1815)].

'Besides our regiment there were the 1st Royals and the Enniskillens, and we were known as the Union Brigade because, you see, it was made up of one English, one Irish and one Scots regiment.

'On the day before the great fight – that was Saturday, for you know the battle was fought on the Sunday morning, the 18th June – we were marched from Quatre-Bras along the road towards Brussels. We thought the Duke was taking us there; but no. In a drenching rain we were told to halt and lie down in a hollow to the right of the main road, among some green barley. Yes, how we tramped down the corn! The wet barley soon soaked us, so we set about making fires beside a cross-road that ran along the hollow in which we were posted. No rations were served that night. As we sat round our fire we heard a loud, rumbling noise about a mile away and this we knew must be the French artillery and waggons coming up. It went rolling on incessantly all night, rising and falling like that sound just now of the wind in the chimney.

'One thing I must tell you: though there were more than 70,000 Frenchmen over there, we never once saw a camp-fire burning all the night until six o'clock next morning. Why they weren't allowed to warm themselves, poor fellows! I don't know. Well, about eleven o'clock that night a fearful storm burst over us. The thunder was terrible to hear. It was a battle royal of the elements, as if the whole clouds were going to fall on us. We said it was a warning to Bonaparte that all nature was angry at him.

'Around the fires we soon fell asleep, for we were all wore out with our long march in the sultry heat of the day before.

'I was awakened about five o'clock by my comrade MacGee, who sprang up and cried, "D– your eyes, boys, there's the bugle!" "Tuts, Jack!" I replied, "it's the horses' chains clanking." "Clankin'?". "What's that, then?" as a clear blast fell on our ears.

'After I had eaten my ration of "stirabout" – oatmeal and water – I was sent forward on picket to the road two hundred yards in front, to watch the enemy. It was day-light, and the sun was every now and again sending bright flashes of light through the broken clouds. As I stood behind the straggling hedge and low beech-trees that skirted the high banks of the sunken road on both sides, I could see the French army drawn up in heavy masses opposite me. They were only a mile from where I stood; but the distance seemed greater, for between us the mist still filled the hollows. There were great columns of infantry, and squadron after squadron of Cuirassiers, red Dragoons, brown Hussars, and green Lancers with little swallow-tail flags at the end of their lances. The grandest sight was a regiment of Cuirassiers dashing at full gallop over the brow of the hill opposite me, with the sun rising on their steel breastplates. It was a splendid show. Every now and then the sun lit up the whole country. No one who saw it could ever forget it.

'Between eight and nine there was a sudden roll of drums along the whole of the enemy's line, and a burst of music from the bands of a hundred battalions came to me on the wind. I seemed to recognise the "Marseillaise", but sounds got mixed and lost in a sudden uproar that arose. Then every regiment began to move. They were taking up positions for the battle. On our side perfect silence reigned; but I saw that with us too preparations were being made. Down below me a regiment of Germans was marching through the growing corn to the support of others who were in possession of a farmhouse that lay between the two armies. This was the farm of La Haye Sainte, and it was near there that the battle raged fiercest. These brave Germans! They died to a man before the French stormed it, at the point of a bayonet, in the afternoon. A battery of artillery now came dashing along the road in fine style and passed in front of me. I think they were Hanoverians; they were not British troops, but I don't remember whether they were Dutch or German. They drew up close by, about a hundred yards in front of the road. There were four guns. Then a strong brigade of Dutch and Belgians marched up with swinging, quick step, and turned off at a cross-road between high banks on the plateau on the most exposed slope our position. They numbered at least 3,000 men, and looked well in their blue coats and orange-and-red facings. After this I rode up to a party of Highlanders under the command of Captain Ferrier, from Belsyde, Linlithgow, whom I knew to belong to the 92nd or 'Gay Gordons', as we called them. All were intently watching the movements going on about them. They, with the 79th Cameron Highlanders, the Forty-second (Black Watch), and First Royal Scots formed part of Picton's "Fighting Division". They began to tell me about the battle at Quatre-Bras two days before, when every regiment in brave old Picton's division had lost more than one-third of its men. The Gordons, they said, had lost half their number and 25 out of 36 officers. Little did we think that before the sun set that night not thirty men of our own regiment would answer the roll-call.

'I seem to remember everything as if it happened yesterday. After the village clocks had struck eleven the guns on the French centre thundered out, and the musketry firing commenced away to the far right. The French were seen to be attacking a farmhouse there in force. It was called Hougoumont. I noticed, just in front of me, great columns of infantry beginning to advance over the brow of the hill on their side of the valley, marching straight for us. Then began a tremendous cannonade from 250 French guns all along the lines. The noise was fearful; but just then a loud report rent the air, followed by a rolling cheer on our side, and our artillery got into action. We had 150 guns in all; but half of them belonged to the Dutch, Germans, or Belgians, who were hired to fight on our side. The French had about 10,000 men more than we had all that day, till, late in the afternoon, the Prussians arrived with 40,000 men to help us. I was now drawn back and joined our regiment, which was being moved forward to the left under better cover near a wood, as the shot and shell were flying about us and ploughing up the earth around.

'We had hardly reached our position when a great fusillade commenced just in front of us, and we saw the Highlanders moving up towards the road to the right. Then, suddenly, a great noise of firing and hisses and shouting commenced, and the whole Belgian brigade, of those whom I had seen in the morning, came rushing along and across the road in full flight. Our men began to shout and groan at them too. They had bolted almost without firing a shot, and left the brigade of Highlanders to meet the whole French attack on the British left centre. It was thought that the Belgians were inclined towards Napoleon's cause, and this must account for their action, as they have shown high courage at other times.

'Immediately after this, the General of the Union Brigade, Sir William Ponsonby, came riding up to us on a small bay hack. I remember that his groom with his chestnut charger could not be found. Besides him was his aide-de-camp, De Lacy Evans. He ordered us forward to within 50 yards of the beech-hedge by the roadside. I can see him now in his long cloak and great cocked hat as he rode up to watch the fighting below. From our new position we could descry the three regiments of Highlanders, only 1,000 in all, bravely firing down on the advancing masses of Frenchmen. These numbered thousands, and those on our side of the Brussels road were divided into three solid columns. I have read since that there were 15,000 of them under Count D'Erlon spread over the clover, barley, and rye fields in front of our centre, and making straight for us. Then I saw the Brigadier, Sir Denis Pack, turn to the Gordons and shout out with great energy, "92nd, you must advance! All in front of you have given way." The Highlanders, who had begun the day by solemnly chanting "Scots wha hae" as they prepared their morning meal, instantly, with fixed bayonets, began to press forward through the beech and holly hedge to a line of bushes that grew along the face of the slope in front. They uttered loud shouts as they ran forward and fired a volley at twenty yards into the French.

'At this moment our General and his aide-de-camp made off to the right by the side of the hedge; then suddenly I saw De Lacy Evans wave his hat, and immediately our colonel, Inglis Hamilton [of Murdestone, Lanarkshire], shouted out, "Now then, Scots Greys, charge!" and, waving his sword in the air, he rode straight at the hedges in front, which he took in grand style. At once a great cheer rose from our ranks, and we too waved our swords and followed him. I dug my spear into my brave old Rattler, and we were off like the wind. Just then I saw Major Hankin fall wounded. I felt a strange thrill run through me, and I am sure that my noble beast felt the same, for, after rearing for a moment, she sprang forward, uttering loud neighings and snortings, and leapt over the holly-hedge at a terrific speed. It was a grand sight to see the long line of giant grey horses dashing alone with flowing manes and heads down, tearing up the turf about them as they went.

'The men in their red coats and tall bearskins were cheering loudly, and the trumpeters were sounding the "Charge". Beyond the first hedge the road was sunk between high, sloping banks, and it was a very difficult feat to descend without falling; but there were very few accidents, to our surprise.

'All of us were greatly were greatly excited, and began crying, "Hurrah, 92nd! Scotland for ever!" as we crossed the road. For we heard the Highland pipers playing among the smoke and firiong below, and I plainly saw my old friend Pipe-Major Cameron standing apart on a hillock coolly playing "Johnny Cope, are ye waukin' yet?" in all the din.'

(It should not be necessary to point out that the song was a Jacobite marching satire commemorating a victory over the UK troops in 1745, when the Camerons were loyal adherents to James VIII of Scotland and his son Charles.)

'Our colonel went on before us, past our guns and down the slope, and we followed; we saw the Royals and Enniskillens clearing the road and hedges at full gallop away to the right.

'Before me rode young Armour, our rough-rider from Mauchline (a near relative of Jean Armour, Robbie Burns's wife), and

Sergeant Ewart, at the end of the line, beside our cornet, Kinchant. I rode in the second rank. As we tightened our grip to descend the hillside along the corn, we could make out the feather bonnets of the Highlanders, and heard the officers crying out to them to wheel back by sections. A moment more, and we were among them. Poor fellows! Some of them had not time to get clear of us, and were knocked down. I remember one lad crying out, "Eh! But I didna think ye wad ha'e hurt me sae".

'They were all Gordons, and as we passed through them, they shouted, "Go at them, the Greys! Scotland for ever!" My blood thrilled at this, and I clutched my sabre tighter. Many of the Highlanders grasped our stirrrups, and, in the fiercest excitement dashed with us into the fight. The French were uttering loud, discordant yells. Just then I saw the first Frenchman. A young officer of Fusiliers made a slash at me with his sword, but I parried it and broke his arm; the next second we were in the thick of them. We could not see five yards ahead for the smoke. I stuck close by Armour; Ewart was now in front.

'The French were fighting like tigers. Some of the wounded were firing at us as we passed; and poor Kinchant, who had spared one of these rascals, was himself shot by the officer he had spared. As we were sweeping down a steep slope on the top of them, they had to give way. Then those in front began to cry for 'quarter', throwing down their muskets and taking off their belts. The Gordons at this rushed in and drove the French to the rear. I was now in the front rank, for many of ours had fallen. It was here that Lieutenant Trotter, from Morton Hall, was killed by a French officer after the first rush on the French. We now came to an open space covered with bushes, and then I saw Ewart, with five or six infantry men about him, slashing right and left at them. Armour and I dashed up to these half-dozen Frenchmen, who were trying to escape with one of their standards. I cried to Armour to 'Come on!' and we rode at them. Ewart had finished two of them, and was in the act of striking a third man who held the Eagle; next moment I saw Ewart cut him down, and he fell dead. I was just in time to thwart a bayonet-thrust that was aimed at the gallant sergeant's neck. Armour finished another of them.'

Our host pointed out to his little company of intent listeners a print of the well-known picture of the incident which hung on the wall, and of which he was very proud; [evidently *The Fight for the Standard* by Richard Ansdell (1815–85)] then he continued:

'Almost single-handed, Ewart had captured the Imperial Eagle of the 45th 'Invincibles', which had led them to victory at Austerlitz and Jena. Well did he merit the commission he received at the hands of the Prince Regent shortly afterwards, and the regiment has worn a French Eagle ever since.

'We cried out, "Well done, my boy!" and as others had come up, we spurred on in search of a like success. Here it was that we came upon two batteries of French guns which had been sent forward to support the infantry. They were now deserted by the gunners and had sunk deep into the mud.

'We were saluted with a sharp fire of musketry, and again found ourselves beset by thousands of Frenchmen. We had fallen upon a second column; they were also Fusiliers. Trumpeter Reeves of our troup, who rode by my side, sounded a "Rally", and our men came swarming up from all sides, some Enniskillens and Royals being amongst the number. We at once began a furious onslaught on this obstacle, and soon made an impression; the battalions seemed to open out for us to pass through, and so it happened that in five minutes we had cut our way through as many thousands of Frenchmen.

'We had now reached the bottom of the slope. There the ground was slippery with deep mud. Urging each other on, we dashed towards the batteries on the ridge above, which had worked such havoc on our ranks. The ground was very difficult, and especially where we crossed the edge of a ploughed field, so that our horses sank to the knees as we struggled on. My brave Rattler was becoming quite exhausted, but we dashed ever onwards.

'At this moment Colonel Hamilton rode up to us crying, "Charge! Charge the guns!" and went off like the wind up towards the terrible battery that had made such deadly work among the Highlanders. It was the last we saw of our colonel, poor fellow!

His body was found with both arms cut off. His pockets had been rifled. I once heard Major Clarke tell how he saw him wounded among the guns of the great battery, going at full speed, with the bride-relics between his teeth, after he had lost his hands.

'Then we got among the guns, and had our revenge. Such slaughtering! We sabred the gunners, lamed the horses, and cut their traces and harness. I can hear the Frenchmen yet, crying "Diable!" when I struck at them, and the long-drawn hiss through their teeth as my sword went home. Fifteen of their guns could not be fired again that day. The artillery drivers sat on their horses weeping again as we went among them}; they were mere boys, we thought.

'Rattler lost her temper and bit and tore at everything that came in her way. She seemed to have got new strength. I had lost the plume of my bearskin just as we went through the second infantry column; a shot had carried it away. The French infantry were rushing past us in disorder on their way to the rear, Armour shouted at me to dismount, for old Rattler was badly wounded. I did so just in time, for she fell heavily the next second. I caught hold of a French officer's horse and sprang on her back and rode on.

'Then we saw a party of horsemen in front of us on the rising ground near a farmhouse. There was "the Little Corporal" himself, as his veterans called Bonaparte. It was not until next night, when our men had captured his guide, the Belgian La Coste, that we learned what the Emperor thought of us. On seeing us clear the second column and commence to attack his eighty guns on the centre, he cried out, "Those terrible Greys, how they fight!" for you know that all our horses, dear old Rattler among them, fought that day as angrily as we did. I never saw horses become so ferocious, and woe betide the blue coats that came in their way! But the noble beasts were now exhausted and quite blown, so that I began to think it was time to get clear away to our own lines again.

'But you can imagine my astonishment when down below, on the very ground we had crossed, appeared in full gallop a couple of regiments of Cuirassiers on the right, and away to the left a

regiment of Lancers. I shall never forget the sight. The
Cuirassiers, in their sparkling steel breastplates and helmets,
mounted on strong black horses, with great blue rugs upon the
croups, were galloping towards me, tearing up the earth as they
went, the trumpets blowing wild notes in the midst of the
discharges of grape and canister shot from the heights. Around
me there was one continuous noise of clashing arms, shouting of
men, neighing and moaning of horses. What were we to do?
Behind us we saw masses of French infantry with tall fur hats
coming up at the double, and between us and our lines these
cavalry. There being no officers about, we saw nothing for it but to
go straight at them and trust to Providence to get through. There
were half-a-dozen of us Greys and about a dozen of the Royals
and Enniskillens on the ridge. We all shouted, "Come on, lads;
that's the road home!" and, dashing our spurs into our horses'
sides, set off straight for the Lancers. But we had no chance. I
saw the lances rise and fall for a moment, and Sam Tar, the
leading man of ours, go down amid the flash of steel. I felt a
sudden rage at this, for I knew the poor fellow well; he was a
corporal in our troop. The crash as we met was terrible; the horses
began to rear and bite and neigh loudly, and then some of our
men got down among their feet, and I saw them trying to ward off
the lances with their hands. Cornet Sturges of the Royals – he
joined our regiment as lieutenant a few weeks after the battle
– came up and was next me on the left, and Armour on the right.
"Stick together, lads!" we cried, and went at it with a will, slashing
about us left and right over our horses' necks. The ground around
us was very soft, and our horses could hardly drag their feet out
of the clay. Here again I came to the ground, for a Lancer finished
my new mount, and I thought I was done for. We were returning
past the edge of the ploughed field, and then I saw a spectacle I
shall never forget. There lay brave old Ponsonby, the general of
our Union Brigade, beside his little bay, both dead. His long,
fur-lined coat had blown aside, and at his hand I noticed a miniature
of a lady and his watch; beyond him, our Brigade-Major, Reignolds
of the Greys. They had both been pierced by the Lancers a few
moments before we came up. Near them was lying a lieutenant of

ours, Carruthers of Annandale. My heart was filled with sorrow at this, but I dared not remain for a moment. It was just then I caught sight of a squadron of British Dragoons making straight for us. The Frenchmen at that instant seemed to give way, and in a minute more we were safe! The Dragoons gave us a cheer and rode on after the Lancers. They were the men of our 16th Light Dragoons [under Colonel John Hay, afterwards Colonel-in-Chief of the 79th Cameron Highlanders], of Vandeleur's Brigade, who not only saved us but threw back the Lancers into the hollow.

'How I reached our lines I can hardly saw, for the next thing I remember is that I was lying with the sole remnants of our brigade in a position far away to the right and rear of our first post. I was told that a third horse that I caught was so wounded that she fell dead as I was mounting her.

'Wonderful to relate Rattler had joined the retreating Greys, and was standing in line riderless when I returned. You can imagine my joy at seeing her as she nervously rubbed shoulders with her neighbours. Major Cheney (who had five horses killed under him) was mustering our men, and with him were Lieutenant Wyndham afterwards our colonel [the last survivor among the Greys' officers, whose funeral Dickson attended in 1872 in the Tower of London, where he had been the Keeper of the Crown Jewels for twenty years] and Lieutenant Hamilton [son and heir of General John Hamilton of Dalzell, Lanarkshire, and father of Lord Hamilton], but they were both wounded. There were scarcely half a hundred of the Greys left out of the three hundred who rode off half an hour before. [We lost 16 officers out of 24 in the field.] How I escaped is a miracle, for I was through the thick of it all, and received only two slight wounds, one from a bayonet and the other from a lance, and the white plume of my bearskin was shot away. I did not think much of the wounds at the time, and did not report myself; but my poor Rattler had lost much blood from a lance-wound received in her last encounter.

'Every man felt that the honour of our land was at stake, and we remembered that the good name of our great Duke was entrusted to us too; but our main thought was, "What will they say of us at home?" It was not till afterwards that we soldiers learned what the Union Brigade had done that day, for a man in the fighting-ranks sees little beyond the sweep of his own sword. We had pierced three columns of 15,000 men, had captured two Imperial Eagles and had stormed and rendered useless for a time more than forty of the enemy's cannon. Besides, we had taken nearly three thousand prisoners, and, when utterly exhausted, had fought our way home through several regiments of fresh cavalry. That, my friends, is why, from the Prince Regent to the poorest peasant, from the palace to the lowliest cottage, the name of the Union Brigade was honoured throughout the land.'

When the sergeant had finished his story the toddy had cooled in the tumblers; but there was time to fill them and drink 'Long Life to the Sergeant' and to the Union Brigade of our own time, whose charge on Balaklava Day proved that they were worthy successors of the Heroes of Waterloo.

Perhaps, but they were led infinitely worse.

Sergeant-Major Dickson's story comes to us an uncertain remove beyond the immediacy of Sergeant Robertson. There is avowedly at least one other voice in the telling of it, and possibly more hands than one in writing it down and preparing it for publication or at least for archiving. Nevertheless it asserts its own authenticity. The Sergeant-Major has perhaps a wider eye in his authority than the Sergeant. Both of them get us thoroughly into the middle of things, get isolation and bewilderment across when required, and give their cameo shot, even of the leading protagonists, with clarity and without fuss. The intrusion of the Crimean War in the editor's contextualisation is an unintentional reassertion of authenticity. That editor's anxiety to make much of the Crimea in the midst of the actually far greater and nobler tale of Waterloo, reasserts the domination of the Sergeant-major's narrative, because it is not intruded into what he has to tell, leaving the feeling the note-taking was spontaneous though possibly shared by more than one auditor, and while the smooth flow is admirable, it is likely that the text was subsequently checked with the speaker. Above all it passes the chief test: we are there. The old soldier reminiscing may have been an obvious vehicle for fictionists to appropriate, as Conan Doyle's Brigadier Gerard stories brought to a fine art. How far its use by or for Sergeant-Major Dickson was fictional may be insoluble, but the core seems reliable enough.

3

Doctors

The Scottish Enlightenment lasted longer than its European counterpart, having no revolution or Napoleon to guillotine it, and if it was prolonged visibly in any one area it was medicine. Conan Doyle as an Edinburgh medical student in 1876–81 accumulated enough surviving data from it to create Sherlock and Mycroft Holmes, Professor Challenger, and probably Professor Moriarty. Edinburgh medical products flourished far beyond Edinburgh limits. What Waterloo offered above all to the enlightened scientist was a field seeping with data living and dead.

Charles Bell (1774–1842), surgeon and artist, whirled round to his brother-in-law and disciple John Shaw (1792–1827) on the news of Waterloo (according to the anonymous editor of his *Letters* (1870)): 'Johnnie! How can we let this pass? Here is such an occasion of seeing gun-shot wounds come to our very door. Let us go!' They were off to Dover on 26 June whence he wrote to his wife:

DOVER

26 June 1815

My dear love, here we are sitting by the seaside, all bright as a cloud in sunshine; wind adverse, but fine gentle breeze. We are waiting for a king's messenger.

We are all well; Johnnie the most tired. Depend upon it I have good stamina when my mind is engaged. Nothing but idleness affects me; say does it ever? Thanks to my own dear May for letting me off so well; not too little for a fond husband, not too much for a sensible wife. Remember my advice about driving, etc, and the roses in the cheeks, and all that...

OSTEND

29 June

We came in here at six o'clock. Poor C. [himself], two days and nights without a morsel [presumably to avoid sea-sickness on a sailing-ship]. What a pity! However, I am at this moment dressed, fresh and strong. The harbour and town exceedingly like – Ostend. We have no news. One fellow tells us Buonaparte cut him troat, and Vellington in Paris, and Buonaparte head up street on a pike, 10,000 men! What this means I know not, nor care, so that the war be over. We must to breakfast.

C.B.

[From CB's pencilled note-book:]

Dover, 26 June 1815. Came from London in the evening, amidst the utmost bustle; the fight at the Courier office a mimic representation of the battle of Mont St John. A jolly scene of English husbandmen; everything national has now a double interest – one likes the more to see them.

Ostend, 29 June 1815. We have passed all other parties. Greatly less interest here on public matters than in England. A want of life, or of formed opinions in the expression of the people.

Ghent. By far the most beautiful town I have ever seen, fully answering the notion of an old town of the Pays Bas – a dream of spires and pinnacles quite to my taste.

Passports? Non, nous non avons pas! Non.

We ought to have, for to come into Flanders, and through fortified towns, one must otherwise in time of war expect fierce interruptions, which, as now, take the agreeable reflection and right tone from us. [Editor notes: They set off immediately after hearing the news of the battle, and the only passports they thought of were surgical instruments! Which John Shaw shook in the faces of the officials. These passed them.]

Nine o'clock. On reaching Brussels, how extraordinary! We enter by a very dirty part of the town, low; also a rag market, a fish market, a fair, a great concourse. The wounded everywhere conspicuous, dragging, pale; a great many wounded in the head. These, of course, move about; and on the doors 5 blesses, and on passing the church – God! – what a piece of perspective!

Brussels, 30 June 1815. A little while I must write before going to bed. But how? – in such a crowd of images – after such fatigue – fatigue which I did not know I could have undergone. I have been chiefly in four great hospitals; but I must not speak of them, only of the town, as a common traveller. It would be natural to say, 'how stupid; how supine.' But no! the excitement and the exertions have been the greatest possible; but it is past, and I must not wonder if I do not see what, as a new comer, I feel. I must not wonder that there are smiles, and that people transact their business as in common days. I understand the people have … Oh! It is too much – my head!.

1 July, 5 o'clock, A.M. I, who cannot exert myself at home without my full eight hours sleep, cannot rest after four hours. I write this in bed, for I must at least spare my feet.

The force with which the cuirassiers came on is wonderful. Here is an officer wounded; a sword pierced the back and upper parts, went through the wood-work and leather of the saddle, and entered the horse's body, pinning the man to the horse.

–, who only repeats what others of a certain rank say, remarked to me that Wellington might well be alarmed for his own impetuosity. While the newspapers announced Buonaparte from Paris, he said, 'If I can only permit him to come on for enough to show his intention distinctly, and that he thus stands committed, I think I can do for him.' By-the-bye, I never can hear of Wellington saying a thing well, but rather as if he affected a kind of boyish slang. Either there was a complete surprise, or these three Scottish regiments were sacrificed to this intention, for they were successively cut down as they marched up, one regiment after another. Wellington said during the battle, 'It will all be over by-and-by'. He expected the flank movement of the Prussians; they did on come till five hours after they were expected.

It was thought that we were prepared for a great battle, yet here we are, eleven days after it, only making arrangements for the reception of the wounded. The expression is continually heard, 'We were not prepared for this'.

On what then did the success of the day mainly depend? On the intrepid fighting, or the bottom of the British soldier. ['bottom' here means 'resolution']

A colonel of the Greys was wounded in the thigh, and his horse killed. The horse fell jupon him, and he was kept staked there, a few feet from the muzzle of the guns; he heard his men swearing, and wondering at the fighting of the French. He was not safe until the British began to play their rockets on the French.

3 July, Monday morning. I could not sleep for thinking of the state of the wounded French. 'Pansez! [Bandage!] Pansez, majeur docteur', 'or 'coupez [cut], coupez', sounded in my ears. I rose at four o'clock, and wrote to the surgeon-in-chief, and have taken on me to perform all the capital operations on the wounded French – no small effort. I must, therefore, resign other objects, having, however, done more than I expected.

By having the names of the hospitals, their surgeons, and the list of cases, my other objects may be obtained at home. Sleep I must have – the want of it alarms me...

After three days of the most severe application to the duties I had undertaken (of which see my note book), I rested, but found myself again so called upon by the interest of the cases, that I could not set out. Thursday I gave to the field, and a few cases of officers, whom I saw in the evening.

[Anon. ed: annotates:

The surgical notes were inserted in another note book, accompanied by Charles Bell's sketches of the wounded. These sketches, afterwards reproduced in water-colours, excelled in form and effect any professional paintings hitherto attempted. Many of them, together with some in oil, are now along with the Windmill Street Museum, in the College of Surgeons [now located in Nicolson St.] Edinburgh; others in the University College of [Gower St] London ; and seventeen were presented by his widow, in 1867, to the Royal Hospital, Netley, along with the note-book.]

The Field of Waterloo

From a little beyond Brussels the road is through the forest of Soignies – 15 miles to Waterloo; the road unincumbered, but by horrid smells. Waterloo, a quiet little village, in which all is already quiet and tranquil.

Here we mounted – the forest still continuing. We at last emerged from the avenue, the field of battle opening before us to our right and left. The first note of our arrival on the scene was the disorder on the left hand side of the road by the bivouac of horses, I suppose the draught-horses of the ammunition. A little further on we saw collected 132 pieces of fine French guns, I think of 12 and six long field pieces, and ten-inch howitzers – beautiful cannon. Some of these were cast since Buonaparte's return, some in the time of Louis [XVIII], and some had 'Liberty and Equality' inscribed on them.

Here we took guides, and turned off to the left of the road to Nivelles. Immediately on the right of the road there had been a tug of war, from the ground cut with hoofs and wheels, and the remains of ammunition. We advanced along the plateau to the centre of the British position. Along the whole brow of the elevated ground were many recently buried, very, very many graves, arms, knapsacks, hats, letters, books. It is inconceivable the numbers of such things strewed about. Riding over this hill we looked down upon Hougoumont. We returned to the farm of La Haye, where the Brunswickers kept possession for the greater part of the day; were destroyed, and the house battered with bullets. Ascending the plateau of – we again descended to the right of his position upon the form of Hougoumont. We walked round the narrow lane behind it, and entered where the Guards died. This beautiful farm, a complete thing, was set fire to by the rockets; it is burned and a ruin, all but one little corner, on which is written 'the quarters of General Byng'.

The gate towards the south, and looking to the position of Buonaparte, is shattered with shot. The Guards here cut down the trees in front; some of the standing trees have 60 shot in them; the ground is ploughed and the trees cut by shot. In rear of this position is a great heap of reeking bones, probably from the collection of the Guards. In front, and at the south gate within the wood, a very large heap of buried bodies; the French were repulsed in their repeated attacks upon this point.

Passing through the little wood which surrounds the farm-house, which is like a little part of forest scenery, the road or avenue leading through it, we come to the ditch without where the French had lain in great strength. The ground was trodden down, the corn quite laid.

From the farm of Hougoumont we rode over rising ground, covered with standing corn, and through the field we could still observe the movements of the French, making streets through the fields, leaving the corn neat, cut as it were, no struggling. They must have moved on in deep column and in numbers, completely to beat the corn into the ground. About half of ascent brought us to the position of Buonaparte.

This is the highest ground in the Pays Bas. A noble expanse is before the eye, and the circumstance of the ground still imprinted with the tyrant's foot, the place where the aides-de-camp galloped to and fro, the whole extent of this important field under the eye, fill the imagination.

I climbed up one of the pillars of the scaffolding, as I was wont to do, after birds-nests, but I found me more heavy. We got a ladder from the farm court; it reached near the first platform. I mounted and climbed with some difficulty; none of the rest would venture, so I feel rather youthful.

The view magnificent, I was only one-third up the machine, yet it was a giddy height. Here Buonaparte stood surveying the field. What name for him but – Macbeth, a man who stands alone. [The allusion here is not to King Macbeth of Scotland (c. 1005–1057 rgd

1040–57) but to Shakespeare's absurdly fanciful masterpiece play where near his death Macbeth says

> They have tied me to a stake; I cannot fly,
> But bear-like, I must fight the course. (V. vii.1-2.)]

There is something magnificent in this idea; then, exalted to a giddy height; and how much further to fall than to the ground? His friends dispersed, his squadron broken, all in deroute; and well he knew – for he seems to know mankind well – he knew the consequences.

He must have turned to the right of the scaffolding, and joined the road, the Chaussee, a little to the side of La Belle Alliance. There he must have met the wreck of his forces. A little further on the road his carriage was found.

This position of Buonaparte is most excellent; the machine had been placed by the side of the road, but he ordered it to be shifted. The shifting of this scaffolding shows sufficiently the power of confidence and the resolution of the man. It is about 60 feet in height. I climbed upon it four times the length of my body, by exact measurement, and this was only the first stage. I was filled with admiration of a man of his habit of life, who could stand perched on a height of 65 feet above everything, and contemplate, see, and manage such a scene. Already silence dwells here; for although it is midday, and the sun bright and all shining in gladness, yet there is a mournful silence contrasted with the scene which has been so recently acting. No living thing is here – no kites, no birds of any kind; nothing but a few wretched women and old men, scattered on a height at a distance, and who are employed in gathering balls.

We descended towards the south-east, crossing the road from Genappes. On a rising-ground to the right of the road must have been the bivouac of the French before the battle – the fields quite broken down, ox-heads, turnips, veal, pigs, sheep, half-mangled and eaten, sticks and the fires and comforts snatched, for the place indicates an immense mass of men in peaceable possession. Where there are the marks of men further towards

Waterloo, there are marks of struggle, loss, and deroute. We now crossed the road, and making a circle round the cottage of La Belle Alliance, came upon the ground occupied by the French during the battle en potence.

From this, down the hill, opposite the British heights, there has been much destruction of life. The balls are thickly strewn; the letters, books, caps, halters, pack-saddles, etc, cover the whole ground. The Prussians must have broken in here, and the marks of the horses' hoofs all in direction to the Chaussee of Genappes.

Picking up these letters, you are at once carried home to the cottage of the poor fellow who fell. It is a letter from his father or his mother. We found letters which he had received when he was in Spain. There seems to have been a little book of manoeuvres which is the code of the French soldiers. We found many. I picked up one stained with blood. I shall preserve it for the sake of the commentary written in the annals of this bloody day.

Every French soldier carries a little book of the receipt of pay, without which he cannot receive anything. It is a printed form, and in the beginning is a code of military punishments. It was very remarkable – indeed, most extraordinary – without knowing this, without alighting and examining the books – to find that wherever French had been slain there lay a library in confusion. The letters were all French and German, with very little exception.

We now advanced in the direction of the French attack upon our left. How natural for a Frenchman to anticipate success with such a general looking down upon him! – with the knowledge of such perfect arrangement –such a strength of men who could not be conquered – such an eye and soul directing such an immense force. For we could now judge of it, we had reached the extreme of their right.

In ascending the heights to the left of Mont St Jean, we saw the marks of the great tug of war – the mortal strife – here Ponsonby fell – here Picton – Colonel Hay...

Charles Bell wrote to his brother George Joseph (1770–1843) Edinburgh legal advocate and authority on Scottish bankruptcy:

BRUSSELS

1 July 1815

My dear Brother

I feel the lively interest excited by my present situation as if it were something improperly indulged until I communicate with you. This country, the finest in the world, has been of late quite out of our minds. I did not in any degree anticipate the pleasure I should enjoy, the admiration forced from me in coming into one of these antique towns, or journeying through this rich garden. Can you recollect the time when there were gentlemen meeting at the Cross of Edinburgh? Or those whom we thought such? They are all collected here. You see the old gentlemen with their scraggy necks sticking out of the collars of their coats – their old-fashioned, square-skirted coats, their canes, their hats; and when they meet, the formal bow, the hat off to the ground, and the powder flying in the wind. I could divert you with the resemblances to old Scottish faces among the peasants, but I noted them at the time, and I write to you of things which you will not find in my pocket-book – only of such.

I have just returned from seeing the French wounded received in their hospital; and could you see them laid out naked, or almost so – 100 in a row of low beds upon the ground, tho' wounded, low, exhausted, tho' beaten, you would still concluded with me that these were fellows capable of marching, unopposed, from the west of Europe to the east of Asia. Strong, thickset, hardy veterans, brave spirits and unsubdued, they cast their wild glance upon you – their black eyes and brown cheeks finely contrasted with the fresh sheets, you would much admire their capacity of adaptation. These fellows are brought from the field after lying many days on the ground, many dying, many in the agony, many miserably racked with pain and spasms, and the fellow next to him mimics him and gives it a tune – 'Aha! Vous chantez bien!' How they are wounded you will see in my notes. But I must not have you to lose this present impression on me of the formidable nature of these fellows – as exemplars of the breed in France. It is a forced praise, for from all I have seen and all I have heard of their fierceness, cruelty, and blood-thirstiness, I cannot convey my detestation of this race of trained banditti. By what means they are to be kept in subjection until other habits come upon them, I am convinced that these men cannot be left to the bent of their propensities.

This superb city is now ornamented with the finest groups of armed men that the most romantic fancy could dream of. I was struck with the words of a friend. – E. –'I saw', said he, 'that man returning from the field on the 16th'. (This was a Brunswicker, of the Black or Death Hussars); he was wounded, and his arm amputated on the field; he was among the first who came in; he wrote straight and stark upon his horse –the bloody clouts about his stump – pale as death, but upright, with a stern, fixed expression of feature, as if loath to lose his revenge.' These troops are very remarkable in their fine military appearance; their dark and ominous dress, strong, manly, northern features, and white mustachios,; and there is something more than commonly impressive about the whole effect.

You know how I live at home; I wrote this last night at one o'clock. I was up, writing a lecture on the general arrangement after a battle, at five this morning. I write at night and in the morning, and go into the hospital after breakfast; but when I have taken several sketches and notes I go into a garden in the park, take coffee, and make out my drawing, and look over my observations. In this John Shaw assists, by taking notes of cases. Of news I have not thought since I left England, so that I am a true Belgian.

Before the battle there were many in Brussels known to be disaffected; the friends of the French were many, and in system. During the battle there was a simultaneous movement of alarm everywhere. Four horsemen rode into the centre of the Belgian hospital, giving the alarm that the French had entered; the same occurred in most places. The bridges were broken down, and carts were placed across the roads to make confusion and to prevent retraite; many of those partisans were shot. However, the impression on those officers with whom I have conversed, is, that the people are very grateful for the victory, and the country saved from so formidable a visitation.

Beside a case which I was visiting to-day, lay a woman wounded with gun-shot – French. It is dreadful to visit these wounded French, the perpetual plaintive cry of 'Pansez, pansez, monsieur docteur, pansez ma cuisse. Ah! Je souffre, je souffre, beaucoup, beaucoup, beaucoup.' [Bandage – or dress – my wound. Oh, I am suffering, suffering, so much, so much, so much!]

This is the second Sunday after the battle, and many are not yet dressed. There are 20,000 wounded in this town, besides those in the hospitals, and the many in the other towns; – only 3000 prisoners; 80,000, they say, killed and wounded on both sides.

The text of the letter is given in Bell's *Letters* (perhaps edited by a nephew or niece), and in the *Life of Sir Walter Scott* (1838) by Scott's son-in-law John Gibson Lockhart (1794–1854). Both editors are faulty, exhibiting 19th-century looseness in document reproduction all too well, one silently dropping some portions, the other others, with certain passages common to both but contrasting in detail. Charles Bell's brother, a fellow-advocate of Scott, handed Bell's letter over to him on which Lockhart later commented:

I think it not wonderful that this extract should have set Scott's imagination effectually on fire; that he should have grasped at the idea of seeing probably the last shadows of real warfare that his own age would afford...

Charles Bell, being protected in a suddenly restored peace, could observe Brussels and bring it to life for us in ways time scarcely permitted Napoleon and Wellington, whatever their powers as literary landscape artists. He also contrasts with thousands of more recent professional visitors who seem to miss so much in their self-preoccupation. He was wise in his generation in looking closely at Brussels. 1830–31 would send the House of Orange on their final departure from power over Belgium, the first crack in the victors' European settlement of 1814–15 (other than the vanquished French themselves in 1830 making their own rearrangements from the Bourbons to their Orleans cousin). Being an artist himself however preoccupied with reproduction of wound conditions and their victims he was a peculiarly appropriate conductor of literary inspiration, but Law, Medicine and Literature probably served one another better in Edinburgh than anywhere else. Charles Bell himself, whether in or out of Edinburgh, was an authority in theory and practice linking painting and drawing to professional Medicine. His few remaining days in Brussels showed the interaction of medical, scientific, social and military worlds as few would otherwise have seen them juxtaposed. He told his wife from a suitably reassuring lodging:

2 July 1815

Brussels, Hotel d'Angleterre

...I take up this sheet for you, and to please you give you a few names, because I know you will not be satisfied with a report of hospital cases. Colonel Harris is struck in the shoulder, and must go home. Colonel [Robert Henry] Dick ([1787–1846]) was struck in the shoulder, the ball did not penetrate; he has gone on this morning to the army with the desire to command his regiment in Paris. I had a note from General [[Frederick]] Adam [[1781–1853]], and examined his wound; the ball has penetrated between the bones of his leg; it remains lodged, and will come out some day without the aid of surgery. The next whom I saw were Major General Sir Edward Barnes [(1776–1838)], Captain [William George Keith] Elphinstone [(1782–1842)], Lieutenant Reynolds, and, lastly, whom I like the most, was a perfect little gentleman, Sir Henry Hardinge [(1785–1856)], who has lost his forearm. [Some of these patients went on to roles of importance in imperial Britain, from Elphinstone who would die amid disaster in the First Afghan War for which he bore too much responsibility, to Hardinge who would die as Commander-in-Chief.]

It is hot and fatiguing walking in the Great Square, and I must mind other matters...

In general the wounded are doing well. I believe I shall be taken to any that are not.

There is a pretty girl who stands to sing to a low organ sweet German airs. Oh, you cannot think how I enjoy a little visionary scene, a little romance, and nothing raises the fit so much as these charming foreign airs.

12 o'clock. I must to bed. I was early up, and to-morrow I shall be in the hospital by six o'clock; I ride after dinner. This afternoon I went through the Place d'Armes, and through the park, which is a square, more magnificent than anything you ever saw. Behind the Stadthouse I mounted the old boulevards, the ramparts, and riding thus elevated round the town, saw it to great advantage. I then rode into the famous Allee Verte, where, mingling with the promenaders and horsemen, are cannon stores, and horses bridled to the stakes – a fine martial sight. The canal is here, too, filled with ships with military stores; altogether, to me a new and singular scene. Yesterday afternoon I took a ride towards the south; came round beyond the old fortifications. The Spanish town and wall still remain [since the future Belgium was ceded to Austria in 1715], and over them are seen, not the houses, but the antique rich spires which, illuminated as the sun went down, presented the most picturesque appearance...

Great hurry – many people wanting me – have undertaken to perform all the operations upon the French – two days' work; after which I shall set off, having seen and done so much that I do not think I shall go to Antwerp. Adieu! Then, my home, my house! One letter I find has been stopped at Ostend – the others may have been. I write to say that I am well, and have done more than I contemplated. I meant to say only that I set off from this on Wednesday – in short, I shall be home within the time. I have much to tell you; be kind to yourself. We have had no letters. Again, adieu, my own dear wife,

Yours,

C. BELL

In July 1815, Charles Bell wrote to Francis Horner (1778–1817), Whig MP and co-founder of the *Edinburgh Review*:

My dear Horner,

I write this to you after being some days at home engaged in my usual occupations, and consequently disengaged of the horrors of the Battle of Waterloo. I feel relief in this, for certainly if I had written to you from Brussels, I should have appeared very extravagant. An absolute revolution took place in my economy, body and soul, so that I, who am known to require eight hours sleep, found first three hours, then one hour and a half, sufficient, after days of the most painful excitement and bodily exertion.

After I had been five days engaged in the prosecution of my object, I found that the best cases, that is, the most horrid wounds, left totally without assistance, were to be found in the hospital of the French wounded; this hospital was only forming. They were even then bringing in these poor creatures from the woods. It is impossible to convey to you the picture of human misery continually before my eyes. What was heart-rending in the day was intolerable at night; and I rose and wrote, at four o'clock in the morning, to the chief surgeon, offering to perform the necessary operations upon the French. At six o'clock I took the knife in my hand, and continued incessantly at work till seven in the evening; and so the second and third day.

All the decencies of performing surgical operations were soon neglected. While I amputated one man's thigh, there lay at one time 13, all beseeching to be taken next; one full of entreaty, one calling upon me to remember my promise to take him, another execrating. It was a strange thing to feel my clothes stiff with blood, and my arms powerless with the exertion of using the knife! And more extraordinary still, to find my mind calm amidst such variety of suffering; but to give one of these objects access to your feelings was to allow yourself to be unmanned for the performance of a duty. It was less painful to look upon the whole than to contemplate one object.

When I first went round the wards of the wounded prisoners my sensations were very extraordinary. We had everywhere heard of the manner in which these men had fought – nothing could surpass their devotedness. In a long ward, containing fifty, there was no expression of suffering, no one spoke to this neighbour. There was a resentful, sullen rigidness of face, a fierceness in their dark eyes as they lay half covered in the sheets.

Sunday – I was interrupted, and now I perceive I was falling into the mistake of attempting to convey to you the feelings which took possession of me, amidst the miseries of Brussels. After being eight days among the wounded I visited the field of battle. The view of the field, the gallant stories, the charges, the individual instances of enterprise and valour recalled me to the sense the world has of victory and Waterloo. But this is transient. A gloomy, uncomfortable view of human nature is the inevitable consequence of looking upon the whole as I did – as I was forced to do.

It is a misfortune to have our sentiments so at variance with the universal impression. But there must ever be associated with the honours of Waterloo, to my eyes, the most shocking sights of woe, to my ear accents of entreaty, outcry from the manly breast, interrupted forcible expressions of the dying, and noisome smells. I must show you my notebooks, for as I took my notes of cases generally by sketching the object of our remarks, it may convey an excuse for this excess of sentiment.

Faithfully yours,

C. BELL

Charles Bell, while performing amputations for which no anaesthetic had yet been invented, made and preserved many drawings of military wounds in the aftermath of Waterloo as elsewhere, writing them up in *Surgical Observations* (1816) and subsequently. For once a historian's voracity has its limits. Neither time nor cost will permit any reproduction, and I am thankful, since this is a book I hope will be re-read. Charles Bell's supporting notes are not in themselves repulsive but they are chilling. Messrs Michael Crumplin and Pete Starling in *Scottish Artist at War* (2005) provide us with Bell's artistry in painting and drawing Napoleonic War wounds, and interested readers should go to their authoritative pages, where they add useful quotations from Bell himself such as 'Remember the short cough and the sound of air spurting at the same time from the wound'. Sir Gordon Gordon-Taylor, KBE, pointed out in his *Sir Charles Bell – His Life and Times* (1958) that Bell was in advance of his time in principles of conservative surgery, treating amputation as a final necessity rather than an immediate resort, as was generally favoured. Arguments that 'only five survived out of 35 amputations that he performed' discredit themselves given his having performed only twelve in all. In any case Bell did not even arrive in Brussels until ten days had elapsed from the battle and the cases with which he was most concerned were the French soldiers who had been left to rot on the battlefield for days. Bell, with characteristic honesty, recorded how he felt about the French soldiers as enemies of humanity, and he was trying to save them. The Crumplin-Starling edition of his drawings reproduces notes from Bell alongside one drawing:

> 30th. A l'Hôpital de Gendarmerie. Bleeding: took off the dressing; bleeding stopped. This is a Frenchman, amputated on the field. [French doctors were at work during the battle.] The stump bleeding, it was necessary to open the wound; but it was open and, under the rags, only this clotted mass of charpie on the face of the stump. This wretched man understands a great deal: he keeps his thumb fixed on the compress over the artery: he says that the artery was tied, but 'qu'il est tombé' [that it has fallen, i.e. that it has unwound]. This is a venous haemorrhage, from the veins being compressed. Here is a hospital male, who says, 'well, they cut them like a round of beef'. The limb is directly off; and the whole on the same level; the bone projecting; the skin not protracted. By-the-by, the surface remarkably healthy, and in good state of graduation. Found this quite historical, for it is far behind...

These data were of course noted for possible future publication of resultant theses, but in the general context of Waterloo it reminds us that the Scottish Enlightenment was in part a Christian Enlightenment, flourishing particularly within the University of Edinburgh under the leadership of Principal William Robertson when the Bells were undergraduates. Christ commanded us to love our enemies, and Charles Bell put it into professional practice.

Robert Knox (1791–1862) was another surgeon at work after Waterloo, whence he sneered in relation to secondary amputation that 'only one of C. Bell's lived'. But Bell was in large and sometimes good company there, since Knox's brilliant lectures as extra-mural anatomist cramming pupils for the university were distinguished by incessant derision of what he took to be rivals or barriers to his professional advancement. As assistant surgeon in the army Knox might have access to human data in studying military wounds, and while controversy had driven Bell for a time to London he had more distinguished friends in Edinburgh than Knox, and indeed in 1836 he returned as Professor of Surgery. Knox by that time had been victimised by his open indifference to whether his anatomy subjects might have been murdered or not when his receivership of corpses provided the murder motive in the trial of William Burke. His guilt has been debated, but it is clear he knew enough to know he must not know anything as regards origin of his deceased audio-visual aids. Walter Scott for one denied his right of indifference to possible murder in furtherance of his scientific needs. Knox went free, but after the graduation of the generation of students who devotedly defended him over Burke and Hare, their younger brothers sidled away and he sought refuge in Glasgow and then in London. Whatever he might have said in lectures where in the art of vituperation anything might serve, he made little printed use of Waterloo experience until the end of his life. It cropped up in his *The Races of Men* (1850) an appallingly influential pseudo-scientific treatise which laid the foundations of racist thought and policies for the ensuing century. In fact it should have been studied by alienists. It was understandable that he dislike Irish Catholics after his disgrace arising from Burke and Hare, but it is difficult to make sense of his insistence that the Celts had betrayed Napoleon at Waterloo.

On 24 May 1862 the *Lancet* (a more reputable publication than in the 1820s when it rivalled Knox in scurrility) printed what would be Knox's last article, returning to his reverence for Napoleon's military surgeon Dominique Larrey (1766–1842), supreme master of military surgery whose courageous practice of his art on the battlefield of Waterloo itself won him the admiration of Wellington and the condemnation of Blücher who tried to have him killed when the Prussians took him prisoner (he was pardoned having saved Blücher's son's life).

On a Case of Gunshot Wound of the Cranium, followed by some Remarkable Psychological Phenomena.

By Robert Knox, M.D.

The following case, though by no means unique, yet presents some points of interest worthy, perhaps, of being recorded. The accident occurred on the ever memorable 18 June 1815, soon after which the patient came into my hands, remaining in Bruxelles until the close of the year, when, having in the meantime returned to France, he presented himself at the hospital of the Gros-Caillou, at which my most esteemed friend the celebrated Baron Larrey was then head surgeon.

The treatment of the case whilst under Baron Larrey has been published by him in the first volume of his 'Clinical Records', and as his account is full and succinct I shall here quote it in his own graphic language. What took place whilst the patient was under my care in Bruxelles I shall state afterwards.

Towards the close of the year 1815, a soldier named Louis Manez presented himself at the Hospital of the Gros Caillou. He was twenty-four years of age, and was a brigadier of dragoons. He had been wounded on the 18 of June 1815, at the battle of Waterloo, having been struck by a musket-ball on the left side of the forehead. The ball remained so firmly fixed in the frontal bone, about four or five bones above the left eyebrow, that all the usual means to extract the ball failed, and, the patient refusing to submit to the application of the trephine, it continued there until his death.

I saw him again on 28 May 1824. He was then a sergeant in the 6th Regiment of the Royal Guard. A small portion of the ball had been detached and came away; there remained only a small fistulous wound. He performed his daily duties as a sub-officer with the utmost care, regularity, and precision.

When wounded, he remained for two days and nights on the field of battle without any assistance. He was removed from the field of battle by an inhabitant of Bruxelles, who called in a surgeon, and bestowed every attention on him until he left Bruxelles for the hospitals of Paris.

He had all his mental faculties and bodily strength, with this exception, that he had lost the recollection of substantive nouns. He was instructor in the use of firearms of a company, each individual of which he knew perfectly, but occasionally he forgot their names, as well as other substantive nouns. He gradually also lost the faculty of hearing and of seeing on that side. From the date just mentioned until 10 November 1827, I heard no more of Manez; it was then I learned from my confrere, Dr Cormac, physician to the hospital, that Manez had died in a neighbouring ward in consequence of pulminory consumption.

I had some difficulty in recognising my former patient. His features were entirely changed; his hair had become as white as in a man of 72. Separating the skull-cap from the rest of the cranium, we found:

1. The dura matter adhering strongly to all the internal surface of the cranium, and especially around the wound; the membrane was also much thicker and denser than natural.

2. An excavation of about an inch and a half in diameter by four or five lines in depth at the summit and a little inwards the temporal side of the interior left lobe of the brain. This excavation was lined with a fine reddish membrane. The

depressed portion of the brain was sound, as well as all the rest of the brain.

3. The pedicle of the ball, on which might be seen the traces of the efforts made to extract it, extended, by a few lines, beyond the level of the periphery of the cranium; and the circumference of the orifice by which it had entered the cranium was worn away obliquely from without inwards, as if worm-eaten.

4. In the cavity of the cranium was an osseous eminence formed by the reunion of three or four fragments of the inner table of the skull, united together by an osseous deposit.

I shall now add to this most graphic and carefully-drawn-up history of the case the circumstances which occurred to Manez from the time I first saw him in Bruxelles to the period when I received an order to close the wards of which I had care, and transmit the remaining wounded to France. This took place on and about 25 December 1815.

I first saw Manez in the Hospital of the Gendarmerie of Bruxelles, of the first division of which I had charge until the closing of the hospital. He was an exceedingly handsome man, mild and intelligent; and he used to accompany me during my morning visit to the wounded (all Frenchmen) translating for me the patois of some Basque soldiers whose language I did not readily comprehend. I learned from him that not only the circumstances under which he received the wound, but also many details – by an eye-witness, be it remarked – of the events of that terrible day. Many of these were confirmed by frequent conversations with the French officers whom I attended. From Manez I learned, if my memory be correct, that he was one of that heroic band of cuirassiers, who, if they had been well led, handled, and supported by the infantry, would have decided the action before two o'clock of the 18th, In a last attempt upon our artillery he was riding up a hollow piece of ground under a heavy fire from the English infantry stationed immediately in front. Oppressed with heat, he incautiously raised his helmet for an instant, when he was struck on the left temple by a musket-ball which brought him to the ground. When I first saw Manez in Bruxelles I remarked that he was fast losing power over the left eyelid, which drooped over the corresponding eye; the power of vision, also, of that eye was becoming weaker, and at times he was slightly confused; but he declined all attempts by operation to remove the ball, which I distinctly felt at the bottom of a flatulous wound of no great depth. Under these circumstances he was left to his fate, although it is now clear that the ball ought to have been removed.

I have already alluded to the many conversations I have had with French and English officers who were wounded in that battle, and with the intelligent men (such as Manez) who belonged to the cuirassiers, the Imperial guard, etc; and the conclusion arrived at was, that the cause of the loss of the battle was a mystery which no one could solve. Baron Larrey, in his memoirs, affirms that as early as three or four o'clock in the afternoon traitors were scattered all about, endeavouring to alarm the troops; and the army knew well that Bourmont had deserted his country. But the wounded who returned to France at the close of the year were in good spirits, and talked freely of striking another blow for Napoleon the Great.

This was Robert Knox's last professional publication before his death at the end of that year's December and it is characteristic of him that the final professional question he invited them to consider hopelessly was what won Waterloo. His obvious partisanship for Napoleon looks egocentric, and its corollary, proto-Nietzschean, and it also constitutes a corollary to his responsibility for Burke and Hare – Napoleon in his view was above mere ideas of good and evil, and so, in Knox's estimation, was Knox. However repulsive a figure, Knox at least shows here that he would lose no jot of immense pride regardless of his mid-career misfortune. He reminds us of the human propensity for worship of monarchy, however absurd the object. Napoleon was after all the most successful mercenary general of all time, linked to and using France whose nationality he only enjoyed by the accident of Corsican birth a couple of years after that island was handed over by its master Genoa. Army men read history through the brutal logic of their own profession and Knox as an army doctor evidently enjoyed thinking of himself as one of them, and their Napoleon would have been the heir of Wallenstein (1583–1634) and Marlborough (1650–1722) in ruthless self-interest. He also possessed in superlative degree the vision of the surgeon as ruler of life and death. It was no accident that Conan Doyle should have been fascinated by Napoleon as an object of literature, or that Sherlock Holmes begins as apparently immune from culture and ethics and his brother Mycroft is the research scientist supreme whose interest in a problem is wholly divorced from any interest in the humans giving rise to it. It did not make Conan Doyle a Nietzschean, but his was the even more scientific response, a desire to anatomise Nietzscheans (primeval or otherwise).

As for Knox, we may at least thank him for his genuine interest in one Waterloo medical survivor thus showing some mild symptoms of affection for the patient as well as for his case. It is a faint acknowledgment of regard for humanity from the icy-blooded receiver of goods from Burke and Hare.

4

Walter Scott

Walter Scott's decision to go to Waterloo, occasioned by Charles Bell's letter to his brother, was in its way as scientific and as impulsive as Bell's own. Both wanted research materials. Both thrilled to the echoes of the last epic struggle likely to surface in their times. Both wanted to enrich humanity. Both believed in the importance of ordinary people. Both knew that soldiers suffer as well as making others suffer. Both (Scott certainly, Bell probably) had a childlike yearning to have been soldiers (Dr Johnson (1709–84) was syntactically exact in saying every man thinks meanly of himself for not having been a soldier, quite a different examination of conscience from wanting to be one at the time of thinking).

But Scott's epiphany at Waterloo also symbolised the theatrical significance of Waterloo, quite apart from what side one might want to conquer and why, or from the skill of a literary anatomist demanding exercise. Scott had already shown, however pseudonymously, that in *Waverley* he could describe the romantic idealism of insurrection and the destruction of a civilisation. In the great phrase of the great Belgian historian Henri Pirenne (1862–1935) if there had been no Mahomet there would have been no Charlemagne; similarly, if there had been no Waterloo there would have been no Dugald Dalgetty, the master-mercenary of *A Legend of Montrose* (1819). It is not enough to make Dalgetty dependent on Scott's contemporary awareness of Napoleon including the impulse that would later make him Napoleon's multi-volume biographer (1827). Scott needed to be at Waterloo while its megadeaths hung over the air. Everything from human survivors to tiny material objects won his omnivorous attention. Among the relics he accumulated was a crust found in the sporran of a Highland soldier killed at Culloden. Scott became the father of modern social history from the recollections of as many previous generations as he could interview in person or from the recollections of their descendants.

Theatre lay around all this cultural hunter-gatherer work. To a people or its historians conscious of ancient and modern bardic tradition, it began there. Homer or his Celtic equivalent could not write. To win, indeed to enslave, his audience required theatre. The bard might not act out the parts, but he would act out their creator. Scott's own work as a creator was itself created by that. From a lame childhood he listened to his elders from the chimney corner, learned to draw them out, to classify and ultimately to imitate. First he had to recover the dying oral traditions and texts from his surroundings. Then he had to conscript the print which was so rapidly killing his sources, making them self-conscious and self-denigratory, forcing them into cold-blooded modern language contemptuous of its rich parent dialect whether their own ominously formalised or translated in mean restriction from an abundant Gaelic. His own first major break into creative writing, ten years before Waterloo, the six-Canto *Lay of the Last Minstrel* turned above all on whether the narrator would still in his extreme old age be able to perform. And it blends from its introduction of the minstrel in his infirmity and antiquity into the story we almost see willing itself into being from his words and music. And Scott's theatre dominated the 19th century not from any formally dramatic compositions of his own but in innumerable adaptations of the great novels he had begun in 1814 with Waverley. Edinburgh's leading civic theatre the Royal Lyceum would establish itself in 1883 under the actor-manager John B. Howard (1841–95) above all famous in the title-role of *Rob Roy*. Opera chased itself into Scott novels one after another in scripts turning his ironic intellectualism into every conceivable box-office melodrama. In their way the leading protagonists of Waterloo each proclaimed themselves enemies of tyranny, each would be denounced by the others' votaries as tyrants. The very battle itself seemed almost a demand for the greatest encore of all time. One could not leave the action on Napoleon as nursery king in Elba or

Wellington subordinating clauses in Vienna protocols. It might seem a little hard on the soldiers but as Charles Bell realised, Napoleon's troops seemed to want it, however forlorn the hope of the Hundred Days, while Wellington's were not conscripts nor likely to rejoice unduly in the poverty of peace.

And the imminent 19th century urban prospects required it. Trafalgar Square thundered London's salutation to the destruction of Napoleon's challenge to British naval supremacy. Paris proclaimed its ruthless answer in the Avenue d'Austerlitz and the Avenue de Iena. For Scotland's dormant but not extinct capital Edinburgh rounding out its Enlightened self-reinvention, Waterloo Place would fit neatly into space between Princes Street commemorating the Hanoverian candidates for kingship over philosophers, and Regent Road, commemorating the nominal conqueror of the Emperor. The real conqueror, Wellington, sits on his horse Copenhagen with its posterior to the Scottish Record Office gazing somewhat ominously southward diagonally across from Waterloo Place. The names juxtaposed themselves happily and theatrically enough, as post-Union Dublin would acknowledge in adjoining Waterloo Road and Wellington Road as fashionable but quiet gentility for that latest human invention, the Irish bourgeoisie.

Scott set out for Waterloo on Friday 28 July 1815 with John Scott of Gala, Alexander Pringle the younger of Whythank, and the advocate Robert Bruce, by stage-coach to Newcastle, via the fateful field of Flodden where the flower of Scotland in the persons of the King-Emperor James IV (1473–1513) and his warriors were wiped out by an English army. Scott had made that the basis of his verse epic *Marmion* while shrewdly focussing on the later life and death of an English champion, one of the few on his side to die in the battle. He also made his anti-hero militarily courageous but morally doubtful. Byron ridiculed it in his 'English Bards and Scotch Reviewers' having imagined Scott was the author of a demolition in the *Edinburgh Review* of his juvenile poems (Scott had in fact tried to prevent the review's being published). By now Byron had recovered and began turning out Gothic poems and plays with heroes supposedly like Byron but actually like Marmion. Scott good-naturedly insisted to his printer James Ballantyne (1772–1833) that 'Byron hits the mark where I don't even pretend to fledge my arrow' whose generosity does not remove the suspicion that he knew Manfred, the Giaour, and the rest for Marmion's (illegitimate) children. The two met in 1814 and became such friends that Scott thought Byron courteous and kind, and (only partly playfully) suggested to him that he might become a Roman Catholic if he lived long enough. And Scott became as near to a saint in any future Byronic theogony. *Marmion* the poem set a scene and a theme to be adjusted to what Waterloo would provide, regardless of the four centuries dividing it from Flodden. The friendship with Byron is instructive, given their political and religious differences. The past was of greater importance to Scott than the present. He would probably have sympathised with the famous opening to the novel *The Go-Between* (1953) by L.P. Hartley (1895–1972): 'The past is a foreign country: they do things differently there'. The past made by Scott in the course of discovering it gave him gigantic range of sympathies in contrast to his somewhat narrow and even artificial politics, pegged to such a figure as Wellington more for the way he said things than for what he meant. When hinting at the possible future existence of Byron's Catholicism Scott was aware of a faint attraction to the same thing himself. While neither became Catholics their writings frequently showed a far stronger grasp of Catholicism than could be found in most creative non-Catholic writers of their time. Neither would dream of blunting their own rude reactions to what seemed the more obscurantist epiphanies of Catholicism, but in that they shared common ground with independent Catholics such as their common friend Tom Moore. Even the word 'friend' meant far more to each of them than to most contemporaries. Flodden was in the past, Waterloo in the present, but the present could inform the past if students made the past their chief concern. Imagination could inform reality, if great care be taken. Napoleon was not another Marmion but they shared heroic lack of scruples. And Wellington? Scott was of course on Wellington's side, but the battles his characters fought were not simple matters of right and wrong. As a secret fictionist his conceal-ments went far beyond the norm. The present-day Scott as man and sheriff was for the Union. The author of *Waverley* worked his magic by his own absence from the present while writing. It was rather Catholic, after all, to make so much of relics such as a crust of bread in a Culloden sporran.

Scott to his wife from the Harwich Custom House, 3 August 1815:

> My dear Charlotte,
>
> Here we are upon the immediate point of embarkation and while the Custom house people are searching our baggage I take the opportunity to write a few lines. We passd through Cambridge where we stayd a day to see the university which had like to have cost us dear for the packet saild from Harwich yesterday before we came up which had almost delayed us till Saturday. But we have got a nice little cutter as you ever saw to land us at Helvoet. It sails in about ten minutes and we have it all to ourselves which is very snug. I hope to be in Holland tomorrow and so 'My native Land Goodnight'.
>
> I have no letter from you but have left direction should any arrive to send it to Brussels and I hope they will be attentive. Kiss all the babies for me and assure them wherever I go my heart always turns to them and you. I trust they will be very attentive to my instructions about their learning and particularly obedient to you during my absence. And in short I must comfort myself during my absence with hoping you are all as well as I wish you. Believe me ever most affectionately
>
> Yours
>
> Walter Scott

'My native Land Goodnight' came from Byron's masterpiece *Childe Harold's Pilgrimage*, Canto 1, Verse 13. The first Cantos (hinting at its triumphant resolution in later instalments) had appeared in 1812. The Scotts evidently regarded it affectionately as a common target for alternate appreciation and mockery so that it worked as shorthand in dual understanding:

Adieu. Adieu! My Native Shore
  Fades o'er the waters blue.
The Night-winds sigh, the breakers roar,
  And shrinks the wild sea-mew.
Yon sun that sets upon the sea
  We follow in his flight:
Farewell awhile to him and thee,
  My native Land – Good Night.

Byron in fact was a useful alternative poetic voice for Scott to hear in mind approaching Waterloo.

Scott to his wife from Brussels Hôtel de Flandres on 8 August 1815:

My dearest Charlotte

I had your kind letter with the inclosures on my arrival at this town (I should say city by rights and it well deserves the name) yesterday. You have my letters from Harwich and if Marshal MacDonalds letter is to be found you will probably forward it to Paris. Every thing has gone quite well with us except that we were all very sick at sea Bruce and Pringle severely so. We landed at Helvoet on Saturday morning and came that night to Bergen op Zoom a very strongly fortified town. We visited the places where the English attempted to storm it last year but were unsuccessful after losing many men. On Sunday we were at Antwerp and saw the splendid churches of that city. The French have left little but their exterior architecture to boast of for all the fine paintings by Rubens and others were carried to Paris and in this town the birthplace and habitation of the very first Flemish artists we hardly saw a single good picture. But the churches are most magnificent. We saw the effects of General Grahames bombardment last year houses shatterd to pieces vessells sunk in the harbour, etc, etc. [General Sir Thomas Graham (1748–1843), given Freedom of the

City of Edinburgh alongside Scott 1814 and ennobled as Baron Lynedoch but as Whig MP for Perthshire 1794–1807 perhaps a natural target for Scott criticism.] The English are popular here (for their money doubtless) and the people would fain think that Britain would keep them to herself. Yesterday we travelld from Antwerp to Brussells through the richest and most fertile country I suppose in Europe and now coverd with large and ripe crops but every where you see memorials of war, houses dismantled chateaux of the noblesse deserted and gone into disrepair trees cut down and converted into palisades and so forth. But the country will soon recover for though the French took everything they could they necessarily left the soil and I believe only because they could not carry it off. The people always call them Les Voleurs and even the tea-spoons and linen of the beds and tables at the inns did not escape them. One fat dame with tears in her eyes described her set of damask napkins in a tone that would have grieved your very heart. Meanwhile they expect to redeem their losses at the expence of Milords Anglois whose wealth and generosity has no end in their opinion. I believe they regularly charge us about twice as much as their countrymen yet why should we complain when we can dine on a most capital French dinner with two courses and a desert of mulberries cherries of the finest sorts, capital greengage plumbs peaches nectarines, etc and drink Burgundy as much as we please for not quite five shillings a piece. So our travelling is cheap enough and our living hitherto luxurious. But this will have an end for our journey from Mons to Paris will be bad enough. We travell in a long black queer looking hearse of a thing open on all sides but with curtains to draw if it rains which holds us very conveniently. It is drawn by three horses with a driver who shrieks at them like a highland drover pushing on his bullocks. I find no difficulty whatever in making myself understood and even in maintaining a little conversation. Gala also comes on capitally Pringle attends and improves but we have had some capital scenes with our friend Bruce. One night at Bergen op Zoom we had almost killd ourselves with laughing and though the story is *un peu malhonnete* I cannot help writing it down. We had left him somewhat maliciously to expound to the great far Dutch landlady his wish to have some warm water for his feet and accordingly he made her a very long though somewhat confused harangue upon this topic. But it appeard from her answer that he had totally faild in communicating the nature of his wants for it only produced a solemn assurance on the part of the landlady that he should be satisfactorily supplied with a certain bed-room vessell to which she gave in its most popular and broadest name [*pot pour pissèr* or some such, presumably]. You may imagine what an effect this ambigu produced. As for me I even begin to pick up a word or two of Flemish from knowing the German but for the French – bah – I get on like a magpie.

I saw General Adam yesterday and dine with him today. [Adam had been wounded at Waterloo and thus could not accompany him to the battlefield.] Tomorrow I go to the field of battle and am to have his *aid de camp* and a French officer of Bonap[ar]tes *etat major* to expound unto me. The next day I dare say we shall leave Brussells and be in Paris four days after. Nothing could be kinder than Major General Adam he offerred me horses guides every thing in short. I will call on the Duchess of Richmond [hostess of ball on eve of Waterloo] this morning presuming on your information and my acquaintance with others of her family. Kiss all the babies for me. I hope they mind their lessons. Tell Charles I see little boys like him riding in small cabrioles drawn by goats which trot along very knowingly. The dogs are also frequently harnessed to little *brouettes* [hand-carts] but appear to suffer in this hot weather. I am now writing before breakfast. The English garrison about 500 strong are paraded under our windows. The number of wounded officers is very great still though all who can move are gone home or forward to Paris. One fine young lad a Dutchman dined with us yesterday at the table d'hote who was slashd almost to pieces and we see many on crutches or with their arms in slings. We went to the Comedie Francoise last night but saw little company and none *comme il faut* chiefly subaltern officers. There is little temptation to rest here after seeing what is to be seen and the road to Paris is quite open and safe since the surrender of Valenciennes. Compliments to Miss Millar [family governess] and all friends.

Ever yours most affectionately

W. Scott

Scots had developed mastery in the arts of personal diplomacy, useful introductions, information exchange, and wit for charm, diagnosing what new acquaintances might like to hear for their own interests professional as well as personal, and using family and clan links to extent their personal sway. None did it better than Scott, carrying his vast storehouse of knowledge of past and present judiciously rationing its deployment. This was his first European venture, but Scottish cultural imperialism came instinctively to his master-hand. Inevitably he knew a man who knew a man who might prove useful. In this case he knew William Adam KC (1751–1839), attorney-general to the Prince Regent who in 1814 introduced Scott to that future agent in pumping up Scottish tourism from 1822. General Sir Frederick Adam (1781–1853) was his son, who rode at Wellington's right hand around 6 pm during the battle and heard the half-muttered words 'I believe we shall beat them after all'. Wounded shortly thereafter, Adam was still unable to ride but remained in charge of the Brussels garrison whence he could provide Scott with escorts to the stricken field. One of these fellow-Scots was a Major Pryse Gordon (1762–1845) now on half-pay whose interest in Brussels led him to settle there for the next twenty years and publish his *Belgium and Holland, with a Sketch of the Revolution in the year 1830* (1834). By then he was also the published author of *Personal Memories; or Reminiscences of Men and Manners at Home and Abroad, during the last Half-Century; with Occasional Sketches of the Author's Life being Fragments of the Portfolio of Pryse Lockhart Gordon* (1830) whence our next extract:

> Sir Walter Scott accepted my services to conduct him to Waterloo; the General's aid-de-camp was also of the party. He made no secret of his having undertaken to write something about the

battle; and perhaps he took the greater interest on this account to every thing that he saw. Besides, he had never seen the field of such a conflict; and never having been before on the Continent, it was all new to his comprehensive mind. The day was beautiful; and I had the precaution to send out a couple of saddle-horses, that he might not be fatigued in walking the fields, which had been recently ploughed up.

The animal he rode was so quiet that he was much gratified, and had an opportunity of examining every spot of the position of both armies; and seemed greatly delighted, especially with the Farm of Goumont, where he loitered a couple of hours. In our rounds we fell in with Monsieur de Costar, with whom he got into conversation. This man had attracted so much notice by his pretended story of being about the person of Napoleon, that he was of too much importance to be passed by: I did not, indeed, know as much of this fellow's charlatanism at that time as afterwards, when I saw him confronted with a blacksmith of La Belle Alliance, who had been his companion in a hiding-place ten miles from the field during the whole day; a fact which he could not deny. But he had got up a tale so plausible and so profitable, that he could afford to bestow hush-money on the companion of his flight, so that the imposition was but little known; and strangers continued to be gulled. He had picked up a good deal of information about the positions and details of the battle; and being naturally a sagacious Walloon, and speaking French pretty fluently, he became the favourite cicerone, and every lie he told was taken for gospel. Year after year, until his death in 1824, he continued his popularity, and raised the price of his rounds from a couple of francs to five; besides as much for the hire of a horse, his own property; for he pretended that the fatigue of walking so many hours was beyond his powers. It has been said that in this way he realised every summer a couple of hundred Napoleons...

When Sir Walter had examined every point of defence and attack, we adjourned to the 'Original Duke of Wellington' at Waterloo, to lunch after the fatigues of the ride. Here he had a crowded levee of peasants, and collected a great many trophies, from cuirasses down to buttons and bullets. He picked up himself many little relics, and was fortunate in purchasing a grand cross of the legion of honour, but the most precious memorial was presented to him by my wife – a French soldier's book, well stained with blood, and containing some songs peculiar to the French army, which he found so interesting that he introduced versions of them in his Paul's Letters; of which he did me the honour to send me a copy, with a letter, saying, 'that he considered my wife's gift as the most valuable of all his Waterloo relics'.

On our return from the field, he kindly passed the evening with us, and a few friends whom we invited to meet him. He charmed us with his delightful conversation; and was in great spirits from the agreeable day he had passed; and with great good humour promised to write a stanza in my wife's album. On the following morning he fulfilled his promise by contributing some beautiful verses on Hougoumont. I put him into my little library to prevent interruption, as a great many more persons had paraded in the Parc opposite my window to get a peep of the celebrated man, many having dogged him from his hotel.

Brussels affords but little worthy of the notice of such a traveller as the author of *Waverley* [as yet unidentified]; but he greatly admired the splendid tower of the Maison de Ville, and the ancient sculpture and style of architecture of the buildings which surround the Grand Place.

He told us, with great humour, a laughable incident which had occurred to him at Antwerp. The morning after his arrival at that city from Holland, he started at an early hour to visit the tomb of Rubens in the Church of St Jacques, before his party were up. After wandering about for some time, without finding the object he had in view, he determined to make inquiry, and observing a person stalking about, he addressed him in his best French; but the stranger, pulling off his hat, very respectfully replied in the pure Highland accent 'I'm very sorry, Sir, but I canna speak onything besides English'. 'This is very unlucky indeed, Donald', said Sir Walter, 'but we must help one another, for to tell you the truth, I'm not good at any other tongue but English, or rather, the

Scotch.' 'Oh, sir, maybe', replied the Highlander, 'you are a countryman, and ken my master Captain Cameron of the 79th, and could tell me where he lodges. I'm just come in, Sir, frae a place they call Machlin, and ha' forgotten the name of the captain's quarters; it was something like the Laborer.' 'I can, I think, help you with this, my friend', rejoined Sir Water. 'There it is just opposite to you' (pointing to the Hôtel du Grand Laboureur) 'I dare say that will be the captain's quarter', and it was so. I cannot do justice to the humour with which Sir Walter recounted this dialogue.

Paul's Letters to his Kinfolk mentioned by Major Pryse Gordon was a substantial book recording his travels pseudonymously including 60 pages on Waterloo. Although unlike the Waverley novels whose authorship he concealed for a dozen years, it was quickly known as his work, he enjoyed providing an imaginary circle of kinfolk addressed or noted by his imaginary correspondent. Like his master Jonathan Swift (1667–1745) whose works he edited and whose life he wrote between 1808 and 1814, Scott employed and enjoyed layers of deception and humour, and Paul as author of epistles seems a suitably Swiftian identity deliberately suggesting likeness to the apostle Paul, perhaps as symbol of the evangelist but not the deity he proclaims, in this case Wellington (and yet Napoleon however reprehensible or diabolic could never be fully eliminated from divination). *Paul's Letters* remained out of print for almost two centuries until now, but Paul O'Keeffe, the masterly biographer (2009) of the painter Benjamin Haydon (1786–1846) and author of the stimulating and shrewd *Waterloo: the Aftermath* (2014), has reissued it in a fine scholarly (Vintage) edition (2015) releasing our work from providing a necessarily inadequate extract.

Scott to his wife from Chantilly sur l'Oise 13 August 1815:

My dearest Charlotte

I wrote to you last from Brussells and the day before I left that city I had your kind letter with the Duchess's introductions to the heroe of Waterloo and the other inclosures. You have been very active in getting it forward for which I am greatly obliged as the letters may be of some use to me at Paris. I saw the field of battle in great stile accompanied by one or two officers who had been in the field and mounted on a good horse of Colonel Price Gordons. It still exhibits a most striking picture of desolation all the neighbouring houses being broken down by cannon-shot and shells. There was one sweet little chateau in particular called Hougomont which was the object of several desperate assaults and was at length burnd to the ground. The guards who defended it burnd out of the house retreated into the garden of the chateau and making holes through the brick walls fired out from thence upon the French who held a little wood which surrounded the house. There was an immense carnage on this spot and the stench of the dead bodies is still frightfully sensible. A good dog remained in the house and I saw him quite safe attending his master who had made the stables somewhat habitable. I have pickd up some trifles on the field and bought others from the peasants particularly two fine cuirasses which I hope I shall be able to get home. I intend one for the Duke [of Buccleuch] and will keep the other for Abbotsford: I have also a Croix of the Legion of Honour and some other memorials of this dreadful action.

We set out three days ago for Paris in a little low carriage on four wheels which we hired for the journey. It is very convenient and neat enough. Our journey has been safe enough but very singular for this country is neither at war nor absolutely at peace and the number of the allied troops that still pour into it beggars all description. You see Cossacks Hulans Pandours Prussians Austrians Hanoverians Dutch Belgians English and Scotch highlanders on foot on horseback, in waggons and in every possible mode of conveyance all rushing on to Paris. We passed through Valenciennes and breakfasted there though it is still properly speaking in possession of the Bonapartists and is blockaded by the allies. It has been bombarded and was partly injured. Every other town we passd was garrisoned either by Dutch or British or Prussians and often by all three and the appearance of the different uniforms and national dresses makes the oddest contrast in the world. I saw an old Frenchman in the full costume which you see on the stage sitting on a bench with his snuffbox in hand – on the one side of him was a Dutch of German soldier smoking a long pipe on the other an English soldier with a glass of brandy and water. The poor Frenchman cast his eyes from time to time on his two extraordinary companions shrugging his shoulders and uttering deep groans. Indeed the country is suffering to the very hearts core as well as they have deserved it, it is dismal to behold. In every town almost there are symptoms of bombardment or of storm. As for the country although this is harvest season and a fine crop on the ground you hardly see any labourers. All single houses by the roadside have been sacked or burned and many villages have experienced the same sad fate. In those that are left the windows are shut and closely bard down and the pace has the air of a desert. The few men you see look at you with a mixture of jealousy hatred and fear and you cannot talk to a woman but she falls a-crying. The gaiety and spirit of the nation is for the present at least entirely gone and they have a most hopeless and dispirited appearance being as it were struck dumb by the extent of their misfortunes. They are tolerably used by the British but very ill by the Prussians who have much to avenge and to say the truth do set about the task without mercy. Their officers are not much better than the privates. At the Inn at Roye the officers of a Prussian Hussar regiment dined and eat and drank of the best victuals and wine, then orderd out their horses and told mine host they would pay the bill when they came back.

We saw on the road large parties of Bony's soldiers, who are now disbanded. They made part of the garrison of Conde and of all the ruffian figures I ever saw were the most perfectly brutal. They fixd their eyes on us with a strong expression of malevolence and no doubt would have been mischievous had they had a safe opportunity but the road is coverd with patroles of cavalry and infantry. We came to Chantilly through the forest through a worse road than ever was traversed by a wheel carriage having been entirely destroyed by the passage of cannon. This fine place was demolishd in the first fury of the revolution. The magnificent stables alone remain and these are filled with wild Hussar horses kicking screaming and leaping about and with their yet wilder riders jumping yelling and hollowing and playing all the mischief they can and chasing each other with their naked sabres in a sort of fun which looks very like earnest.

PARIS

15 August

Yesterday we arrived here in safety. The town is one great garrison of foreign troops and the English are encamped in the Elysian fields. We ran hastily to the Louvre the Comedie and in the evening to the Palais Royale but my head is too much stund with what I have seen to give you any detaild account of it. The worst is that the spirit of the Parisians seems quite broken. You hardly see a Frenchman of any rank in the public walks or places of amusement and the *Etrangers* armd up to the teeth stump about every where in their heavy boots and with their strange caps and long swords. I saw two Highlanders common soldiers and their wives busy admiring the famous *Venus de Medicis* and criticising the works of Titian and Raphael. Direct to me Hotel de Bourbon Rue de la paix a Paris and write soon. We are very well lodged here. Kiss all the children for me and pat Fifi and puss.

Yours ever,

W. Scott

[*The Letters of Sir Walter Scott*, ed. H.J.C. Grierson XII. (1937), 134-42]

Charles William Henry Montagu Scott (1772–1819) fourth Duke of Buccleuch, eighth Duke of Queensberry, etc, etc, had a friendship with his kinsman Scott perhaps difficult for readers of today following the later 19th century whose snobs crawled to Dukes, and the later 20th century whose snobs sneered at Dukes. When Scott had got up volunteers to resist a possible invasion of Scotland by Napoleon Buccleuch enlisted, and when Scott was caught in a financial trap Buccleuch lent him £4,000. Scott's yearning to dissolve the mutual hostility between Highland and Lowland led him to elevate Lowland clan relationships into something closer to Highland fealty. It is a value of aristocracy that its existence aids the historian in data retrieval, and Buccleuch, however useful militarily and financially in the present, more importantly expedited Scott's cultural voyages into the past. By now friendship was enhanced by anxiety as Buccleuch's health declined (he would die of tuberculosis four years later). So Scott writing to him was more a bard reporting to a beloved chief whom he instructed as well as followed and for whom he feared.

Scott to Buccleuch, August 1815:

My dear Lord Duke

I promised to let you hear of my wanderings, however unimportant; and have now the pleasure of informing your Grace, that I am at this present time an inhabitant of the Premier Hotel de Cambrai, after having been about a week upon the Continent. We landed at Helvoet, and proceeded up to Brussels, by Bergen op Zoom and Antwerp, both of which are very strongly fortified. The ravages of war are little remarked in a country so rich by nature; but everything seems at present stationary, or rather retrogade, where capital is required. The chateux are deserted, and going to decay; no new houses are built, and those of older date are passing rapidly in the possession of a class inferior to those for whom we must suppose them to have been built. Even the old gentlewoman of Babylon [an ironic synonym for the whore of Babylon, i.e. the Roman Catholic Church] has lost much of her splendour, and her robes and pomp are of a description far subordinate to the costume of her more magnificent days. The dresses of the priests were worn and shabby, both at Antwerp and Brussels, and reminded me of the decayed wardrobe of a bankrupt theatre: yet, though the gentry and priesthood have suffered much, the eternal bounty of nature has protected the lower ranks against much distress. The unexampled fertility of the soil gives them all, and more than they want; and could they but sell the grain which they raise in the Netherlands, nothing else would be wanting to render them the richest people (common people, that is to say) in the world.

On Wednesday last, I rode over the memorable field of Waterloo, now for ever consecrated to immortality. All the more ghastly tokens of the carnage are now removed the bodies both of men and horses being either burned or buried. But all the ground is still torn with the shot and shells, and covered with cartridges, old hats, and shoes, and various relics of the fray which the peasants have not thought worth removing. Besides, at Waterloo and all the hamlets in the vicinage, there is a mart established for cuirasses; for the eagles worn by the imperial guard on their caps; for casques, swords, carabines, and similar articles. I have bought two handsome cuirasses, and intend them, one for Bowhill [the Ducal seat], and one for Abbotsford, if I can get them safe over, which Colonel Price Gordon has promised to manage for me. I have also, for your Grace, one of the little memorandum books which I picked up on the field, in which every French soldier was obliged to enter his receipts and expenditure, his services, and even his punishments. The field was covered with the fragments of these records. I also got a good MS. collection of French songs, probably the work of some young officer, and a croix of the Legion of Honour. I enclose, under another cover, a sketch of the battle, made at Brussels. It is not, I understand, strictly accurate; but sufficiently so as to give a good idea of what took place. In fact, it would require 20 separate plans to give an idea of the battle at its various stages. The front, upon which the armies engaged, does not exceed a long mile. Our line, indeed, originally extended half-a-mile further towards the village of Brain-la-Leude [Braine-l'Alleud]; but as the French indicated no disposition to attack in that direction, the troops which occupied that space were gradually concentrated by Lord Wellington, and made to advance till they had reached Hougomont – a sort of chateau, with a garden and wood attached to it, which was powerfully and effectually maintained by the Guards during the action. This place was particularly interesting. It was a quiet-looking gentleman's house, which had been burnd by the French shells. The defenders, burnd out of the villa itself, betook themselves to the little garden, where, breaking loop-holes through the brick walls, they kept up a most destructive fire on the assailants, who had possessed them of a little wood which surrounds the villa on our side. In this spot vast numbers had fallen; and, being hastily buried, the smell is most offensive at this moment. Indeed, I felt the same annoyance in many parts of the field; and, did I live near the field, I should be anxious about the diseases which this steaming carnage might occasion. The rest of the ground, excepting this chateau, and a farm-house called La Haye Sainte, early taken, and long held, by the French, because it was too close under the brow of the descent on which our artillery was placed to admit of the pieces being depressed so as to play into it, – the rest of the ground, I say, is quite open, and lies between two ridges, one of which (Mont St Jean) was constantly occupied by the English; the other, upon which is the farm of La Belle Alliance, was the position of the French. The slopes between are gentle and varied; the ground everywhere practicable for cavalry, as was well experienced on that memorable day. The cuirassiers, despite their arms of proof, were quite inferior to our heavy dragoons. The meeting of the two bodies occasioned a noise, not unaptly compared to the tinkering and hammering of a smith's shop. Generally the cuirassiers came on stooping their heads very low, and giving point; the British frequently struck away their casques while they were in this posture, and then struck at the bare head. Officers and soldiers all fought hand to hand without distinction; and many of the former owed their life to the dexterity at their weapon, and personal strength of body. [John] Shaw [(1789–1815)], the milling Life-Guardsman, whom your Grace may remember among the Champions of the Fancy, maintained the honour of the fist, and killed or disabled upwards of 20 Frenchmen with his single arm, until he was killed by the assault of numbers. At one place, where there is a sort of precipitous sand or gravel pit, the heavy English cavalry drove many of the cuirassiers over pell-mell, and followed over themselves, like fox-hunters. The conduct of the infantry and artillery was equally, or, if possible, more distinguished, and it was all fully necessary; for, besides that our army was much outnumbered, a great part of the sum-total were foreigners. Of these, the Brunswickers and Hanoverians behaved very well; the Belgians but sorrily enough. On one occasion, when one regiment fairly ran off, Lord Wellington rode up to them, and said: 'My lads, you must be a little blown; come, do take your breath for a moment, and then we'll go back, and try if we can do a little better'; and he actually carried them back to the charge. He was, indeed, upon that date, everywhere and the soul of everything; nor could less than his personal endeavours have supported then spirits of the men through a contest so long, so desperate, and so unequal. At his last attack, Bonaparte brought up 15,000 of his Guard, who had never drawn trigger during the day. It was upon their failure that his hopes abandoned him.

(To pause briefly amid Scott's letter to Buccleuch, its classification of the Hanoverians as foreigners illustrates his automatic reference to the past, thinking instinctively of 1715 rather than 1815. To him in 1715 Hanoverians were German invaders, and Stuarts however Francophile and even Catholic were the true kings. It was not a response limited to such rare towering historical intellects such as Scott, or even to Scots of any intellect. Many English people found Hanover at least as alien as they did Scotland, Wales or Ireland, in some cases even more so, despite all being fellow-subjects of George III. As for his remarks on the Belgians, the great Belgian historian and pioneer in medieval economic history Henri Pirenne (1862–1935) practically gave his country its historical dimension in his multi-volume *Histoire de Belgique* (1922–32), and therein declared (vol. 6, 242): 'A Waterloo, les soldats belges fires leurs devoir. Ils combattirent aussi bravement sous les orders de Wellington qu'ils l'avaient fait sous ceux de Napoleon.' (At Waterloo, the Belgian soldiers did their duty. They fought as bravely under Wellington's orders as they had under those of Napoleon.) The happy ambiguities of this formula dispose of the issue. Scott's apparent respect for Jean Baptise La Coste (whom he rendered Dacosta to Buccleuch) starkly contrasts with Pryse Gordon's insistence on his fraudulence, but Paul O'Keeffe (*Scott on Waterloo*, 324) points out that 'Napoleon himself is known to have spoken of his guide in conversation with William Warden, surgeon of HMS *Northumberland*, on St Helena, which

gives credence to at least the broad outline of La Coste's account.'
He does not reproduce Scott's private letters which we now resume
where we paused.)

> I spoke long with a shrewd Flemish peasant, called John Dacosta,
> whom he [Napoleon] had seized upon as his guide, and who
> remained beside him the whole day, and afterwards accompanied
> him in his flight as far as Charleroi. Your Grace may be sure that I
> interrogated Mynheer Dacosta very closely about what he heard or
> saw. He guided me to the spot where Bonaparte remained during
> the latter part of the action. It was in the highway from Brussels
> to Charleroi, where it runs between two high banks, on each of
> which was a French battery. He was pretty well sheltered from the
> English fire; and, though many bullets flew over his head, neither
> he nor any of his suite were touched. His other stations, during
> that day, were still more remote from all danger. The story of his
> having an observatory erected for him is a mistake. There is such
> a thing, and he repaired to it during the action; but it was built or
> erected some months before, for the purpose of a trigonometrical
> survey of the country, by the King of the Netherlands.

[The King in question being the recently installed and created
William I of the House of Orange, whose ancestors had been
Stadtholders. So, whatever the sins of 'Dacosta', he convinced Scott
– correctly – that Charles Bell was wrong about the 'observatory'.
Pryse Gordon probably indicated his suspicions to Scott then or
later, and whether or not Scott came to agree with him in the
course of the next year, the idea of a swindler exploiting public
issues worked on him to aid his creation of Dousterswivel in *The
Antiquary* (1816). 'Bony' was an English nickname for Napoleon,
as 'Nosey' or 'Hooky' was for Wellington, with somewhat greater
physiological accuracy.]

> Bony's last position was nearly fronting a tree where the Duke of
> Wellington was stationed; there is not more than a quarter of a
> mile between them; but Bony was well sheltered, and the Duke so
> much exposed, that the tree is barked in several places by the
> cannon-balls levelled at him. As for Bony, Dacosta says he was

very cool during the whole day, and even gay. As the canon-balls flew over them, Dacosta ducked; at which the Emperor laughed, and told him they would hit him all the same. At length, about the time he made his grand and last effort, the re-doubled fire of the Prussian artillery was heard upon his right, and the heads of their columns became visible pressing out of the woods. Aid-de-camp after aid-de-camp came with the tidings of their advance, to which B. only replied, Attendez, attendez, un instant, until he saw his troops, fantassins et cavaliers, return in disorder from the attack. – He then observed hastily to a general beside him, Je crois qu'ils sont mêlés. The person to whom he spoke, hastily raised the spy-glass to his eye; but B., whom the first glance had satisfied of their total discomfiture, bent his face to the ground, and shook his head twice, his complection being then as pale as death. The General then said something, to which Bonaparte answered, 'c'est trop tard – sauvons nous'. Just at that moment, the allied troops, cavalry and infantry, appeared in full advance on all hands; and the Prussians, operating upon the right flank of the French, were rapidly gaining their rear. Bony, therefore, was compelled to abandon the high-road, which, besides, was choked with dead, with baggage, and with cannon; and, gaining the open country, kept at full gallop, until he gained, like Johnnie Cope, the van of the flying army.

[When reaching the high point of victory Scott's narrative instinctively renews its strength by the great moment in the Jacobite past when General Sir John Cope (d. 1760) commander of the troops sent by Britain to aid Maria Theresia in the War of the Austrian Succession and commander-in-chief in Scotland against Bonnie Prince Charlie in 1745, fled with his troops from the Battle of Prestonpans, resulting in the derisive Jacobite song 'Hey, Johnnie Cope'. Emphasis on the defeated general fleeing from the battlefield became a standard device in epic, notably Macaulay's poem 'The Battle of Naseby' supposedly by a Roundhead Sergeant who mocks the final flight of Charles I from the field, and later by Macaulay himself in his *History of England*, and Arthur Conan Doyle in his historical novel *Micah Clarke* (1889), each describing the much more shameful flight of the Duke of Monmouth (1649–85) while his devoted supporters were still being massacred at Sedgemoor.]

The Marechals followed his example; and it was the most complete *sauve qui peut* that can well be imagined. Nevertheless, the prisoners who were brought into Brussels maintained their national impudence, and boldly avowed their intention of sacking the city with every sort of severity. At the same time they had friends there. One man of rank and wealth went over to Bony during the action, and I saw his hotel converted into a hospital for wounded soldiers. It occupied one-half of one of the sides of the Place Royale, a noble square, which your Grace has probably seen. But, in general, the inhabitants of Brussels were very differently disposed; and their benevolence to our poor wounded fellows was unbounded. The difficulty was to prevent them from killing their guests with kindness, by giving them butcher's meat and wine during their fever.

As I cannot put my letter into post until we get to Paris, I shall continue it as we get along.

12 August – Roye, in Picardy – I imagine your Grace about this hour to be tolerably well fagged with a hard day on the moors. If the weather has been as propitious as here, it must be delightful. The country through which we have travelled is most uncommonly fertile, and skirted with beautiful woods; but its present political situation, is so very uncommon, that I would give the world your Grace had come over for a fortnight. France may be considered as neither at peace nor war. Valenciennes, for example, is in a state of blockade and we passed through the posts of the allies, all in the utmost state of vigilance, with patroles of cavalry and videttes of infantry, up to the very gates, and two or three batteries were manned and mounted. The French troops were equally vigilant at the gates, yet made no objections to our passing through the town. Most of them had the white cockade, but looked very sulky, and were in obvious disorder and confusion. They had not yet made their terms with the King, nor accepted a commander appointed by him; but as they obviously feel their party desperate,

the soldiers are running from the officers, and the officers from
the soldiers. In fact, the multiplied hosts which pour into this
country, exhibiting all the various dresses and forms of war which
can be imagined, must necessarily render resistance impracticable.
Yet, like Satan, these fellows retain the unconquered propensity to
defiance, even in the midst of defeat and despair.

(A nice reminder of Scott's regard for John Milton (1608–74)
regardless of their political differences. Here he expected
Buccleuch to think of *Paradise Lost* (1667) I. 105–09 where Satan
rallies Beelzebub:

What though the field be lost?
All is not lost; th'unconquerable will,
And study of revenge, immortal hate,
And courage never to submit or yield:
And what is else not to be overcome?

Once more it gave him common ground with Byron, while certainly
not sharing Byron's reverence for Milton (see his 'Dedication to
Don Juan'). The idea of Napoleon and his devoted adherents
united as reimbodiment of the Miltonic Satan, gave stature to the
great enemy and hence the very size of the biography Scott would
write in 1825–27, although Napoleonists should remember that
originally Scott included the Emperor's soldiers with himself in
identification with the great anti-hero. Most of the civilians who
had encountered them over a 20-year period must have found
them diabolic enough.)

This morning we passed a great number of the disbanded
garrison of Condé, and they were the most horrid cut-throats I
ever saw, extremely disposed to be insolent, and only repressed by
the conscientiousness that all the villages and town around are
occupied by the Allies. They began crying to us in an ironical tone,
'Vive le Roi'; then followed, sotto voce, Sacre B–, Mille diables, and
other graces of French eloquence. I felt very well pleased that we
were armed, and four in number; and still more so that it was
daylight, for they seemed most mischievous ruffians. As for the

appearance of the country, it is, notwithstanding a fine harvest, most melancholy. The windows of the detached houses on the road are uniformly shut up; and you see few people, excepting the peasants who [are] employed in driving the contributions to maintain the armies. The towns are little better, having for the most part been partially injured by shells or by storm, as was the case both of Cambrai and Peronne. The men look very sulky; and if you speak three words to a woman, she is sure to fall a-crying. In short, the politesse and good-humour of this people have fled with the annihilation of their self-conceit; and they look at you as if they thought you were laughing at them, or come to enjoy the triumph of our arms over theirs. Postmasters and landlords are all the same, and hardly likely to be propitiated even by English money, although they charge us about three times as much as they durst do to their countryfolks. As for the Prussians, a party of cavalry officers dined at our hotel at Mons, eat and drink of the best the poor devils had left to give, called for their horses, and laughed in the face of the landlord when he offered his bill, telling him they should pay as they came back. The English, they say, have always paid honourably, and upon these they indemnify themselves. It is impossible to merchander, for if you object, the poor landlady begins to cry, and tells you she will accept whatever your lordship pleases, but she is almost ruined and bankrupt, etc, etc, etc.

This is a long stupid letter, but I will endeavour to send a letter from Paris. Ever your Grace's truly obliged,

Walter Scott

[Grierson ed., *Letters of Scott*, IV. (1933)]

These letters form the main basis of the first draft of Scott's Waterloo, to be variously worked and expanded into *Paul's Letters to His Kinfolk* and ultimately into the close of the gigantic *Life of Napoleon*. An abridgement of the latter by Richard Michaelis (2014) is now conveniently available in one volume. But Scott's poetic reaction while usefully annotated by Paul O'Keeffe may for once be duplicated here. It was in decline by comparison with his great six-canto miniature epics, notably *The Lay of the Last Minstrel, Marmion, The Lady of the Lake* (1810), and *Rokeby* (1813). His genius was moving to prose and his Waterloo letters were hands running over the keys, as Wilde said of Yeats's early poetry. Yet he needed verse to say what prose letters by himself or by his imaginary Paul could not hope to do: he needed to reach for the sublime. Paul O'Keeffe very rightly says that to be fully appreciated and understood Scott's *The Field of Waterloo* (1815) needs to be read aloud. We have forgotten how to rhyme and take foolish vengeance by deserting those who could.

Scott began the poem announced by that title before a line was written or a sea crossed, with lines from Mark Akenside (1721–1770), 'To the Country Gentlemen of England' (1758). That had rallied its audience to the cause of Britain against France in the Seven Years' War, and did so with invocation of an earlier conflict, the Hundred Years' War. By putting six lines from that citation on his title-page Scott was smoothly recalling English nostalgia for traditions of war against formidable Frenchmen while not having to assert them in person, since Scotland, after all, had been on the French side against Edward III (rgd 1327–77), and Richard II (rgd 1377–99) and (in spirit) against Henry V (rgd 1413–22). 'Valois' was the French dynasty ruling as much of France as it could in the 14th and 15th centuries. Charles d'Albret was Constable of France 1402–11, 1413–15), and was killed leading the French at Agincourt. John de Vere (1313–60) seventh earl of Oxford from 1331, served against the Scots 1333, 1335, 1343, and against the French at Crécy (1346) where the English longbow was decisive, also at Poitiers (1356). James de Audley (c. 1312–1386) served against France at Poitiers. Any 14th-century Mowbray might be intended, though in general they were more conspicuous against the Scots than the French:

> Though Valois braved young Edward's gentle hand,
> And Albret rush'd on Henry's way-worn band,
> With Europe's chosen sons, in arms renown'd,

Yet not on Vere's bold archers long they look'd,
Nor Audley's squires nor Mowbray's yeomen brook'd, –
They saw their standard fall, and left their monarch bound.

Apart from the personal diplomacy needed to skirt Scott's Anglo-
phobe inheritance, the verse singles out the capture of a standard
which comprehends Ensign Ewart and Lifeguardsman Shaw for
two, and Napoleon was symbolically bound by the fate of Waterloo.
King John II (1319–64 rgd from 1350) of France was captured at
Poitiers.

Scott might have felt he needed what support Akenside could
give him in drawing the historical long bow, in any sense of the
term. He had sardonically read the notice in the *Edinburgh
Review* for August 1811 by Francis Jeffrey (1773–1850), partisan
in its notice of *The Vision of Don Roderick*, but fair enough in
opining:

> ... that a prosperous poet has always harder measure dealt him by
> the public, in proportion to his former popularity – that his
> formidable rival is commonly himself – and that in comparing his
> new production with his old, we are exceedingly apt to judge of the
> former by their best passages, and of the latter by their worst...

> His hazards, however, are prodigiously increased, if, in these later
> appearances, he should venture upon a theme with which all the
> vulgar echoes of the country are at that moment resounding: if he
> should undertake, for instance, to celebrate the heroes of the last
> *Gazette*, or the victory for which the bells are still ringing, and the
> Tower guns roaring in our ears. All experience has shown, that
> there can be no successful poetry upon subjects of this description:
> – and there are two very good reasons why this must be so. In the
> first place, the author, in such cases, can never tell his readers
> any thing which they did not know better before; and in the second
> place, he can neither add any ennobling circumstance to the
> certain and notorious truth, nor suppress any vulgar or degrading
> ones with which it may happen to be encumbered. The great
> charm of poetry is, that it places before us the newest and most
> extraordinary objects – and by its vivid colours, and artful

combinations, makes us present, as it were, to the most remote
or fabulous transactions. When it chooses, therefore, to employ
itself on transactions that are actually present and before us
already, in all their detail and reality, it evidently has no scope for
its deceptions – the great end which it aims at producing, has
been already attained, though by more vulgar and ordinary means
– every reader of the authentic narrative, has more facts and more
pictures in his memory, than the most diligent versifier could
venture to put into stanza – and therefore the poetical account,
while it is in danger of disgusting the judicious, by the misapplication
of the common hyperboles of poetry, is almost sure to disappoint
every one by its inadequacy and incompleteness.

Scott had been given due notice that if he chose to write 'The Field
of Waterloo', the *Edinburgh Review* and other kindred spirits
would be waiting for him.

And the vulgar assault upon Waterloo, poetry and public
abounded. Scott got his poem out by the end of October 1815,
his urgency above all being to get rapid profits for the first edition
all of which he had earmarked for the widows and children of
soldiers slain in the conflict. Already publishing house and pot-
house were pushing popular productions. One such coarse comp-
etitor 'Battle of Waterloo' was issued from J. Fraser of Stirling,
together with 'The Bonnet so Blue', and 'Love has Eyes':

> Scots sodgers true, wi' bonnets blue,
>   Did never in our days, man,
> Frae people a', baith great and sma',
>   E'er get so muckle praise, man;
> For wi' their brose, an' tartan hose,
>   They made the French to rue, man,
> The bauld attack which they did mak
>   On Scots at Waterloo, man.
>
> CHORUS: Fall al de ral lal, etc

A philabeg's the Frenchman plague,
    The sight they canna' bear, man,
An aff they rin to save their skin,
    When Highland pipes they hear, man:
But if they chance for to advance
    To fight us ance or twice, man
Our Highland lads cast aff their plaids
    And drive them down like mice, man.

For ten years past a' that did list,
    Have been right sair put tillt, man,
And mony a braw Scots man did fa'
    That wore a tartan kilt, man,
For lang in Spain, wi' might and main,
    They fought owre howes and braes, man,
Our brave lads there did suffer sair
    For want o' meat and claise, man.

Next owre to France they had to dance,
    King Louis for to save, man,
Our mony a man back never cam,
    But in it fand his grave, man;
An' bonnets blue, at Waterloo,
    They suffer'd warst of a' man,
The filthy loons of French dragoon
    Did near hand kill them a', man.

She form'd her there in hollow square,
    Her nainsel to defend, man,
And there she stood 'nang brither's blood,
    Until her life did end, man.
Up cam the Greys wi' trotting pace,
    Ahint the Frenchman's back, man,
Wi' bluid an' woun's they knapt their crowns,
    An' kill'd them in a crack, man.

Our bare-hought boys then cheer'd for joy,
    While on their knees they hurkl'd,
An' loud did praise the Scottish Greys,
    Wha' had their enemies conquer'd,
For, warna them, they'd a' been slain,
    As sure's they were alive, man;
For ilka man was o' the clan,
    The French dogs they had five, man.

Wi' Highland rage they did engage,
    An' fast the Frenchmen wounded;
Here's happy lives to men an' wives,
    An' here's to you an' me, man;
Altho' my sang be very lang,
    A langer sang I've seen, man,
I'll tak' a glass, an' let it pass –
    Huzza! God save the King, man.

To follow Paul O'Keeffe's logic, we lose the value of this if we simply sneer if off as third-degree Burns. Our imaginations have to immerse themselves in a full howff (again, in all senses). The next artefact in the brief compilation from J. Fraser and company is a Jacobite love song purportedly from 1752, which would have been a fully acceptable follow-up in an inn of sufficient sympathies. We might have difficulty in finding or imagining Francis Jeffrey editor and critic of the *Edinburgh Review* immersing his gentility in such surroundings. Scott would have been happily at home and hard at work in them, noting words, song, sentiments, stories, manners, customs, turns of speech. And in his ear the proximity of sexagenarian songs of Jacobite provenance alongside chauvinistic rejoicings for Waterloo would have seemed entirely appropriate. But Scott was not entirely dependent on the possibly declining enthusiasm of the vast public which had welcomed *Marmion*. *The Vision of Don Roderick* had won eager plaudits in a letter from a lady whom he had not yet met, Catherine Dorothea Sarah (1772–1831) Duchess of Wellington, to whom he now dedicated 'The Field of Waterloo', while somewhat defensively adding

It may be some apology for the imperfections of this poem, that it was composed hastily, and during a short tour upon the Continent, when the Author's labour were liable to frequent interruption; but his best apology is, that it was written for the purpose of assisting the Waterloo Subscription.

And then:

I

Fair Brussels, thou art far behind,
Though, lingering on the morning wind,
        We yet may hear the hour
Peal'd over orchard and canal,
With voice prolong'd and measured fall,
        From proud St Michael's Tower;
Thy wood, dark Soignies, holds us now,
Where the tall beeches' glossy bough
        For many a league around,
With birch and darksome oak between,
Spreads deep and far a pathless screen
        Of tangled forest ground.
Stems planted close by stems defy
The adventurous foot – the curious eye
        For access seeks in vain;
And the brown tapestry of leaves,
Strewn on the blighted ground, receives
        Nor sun, nor air, nor rain.
No opening glade dawns on our way,
No streamlet, dancing to the ray,
        Our woodland path has cross'd;
And the straight causeway which we tread
Prolongs a line of dull arcade,
Unvarying through the unvaried shade
        Until in distance lost.

II

A brighter, livelier scene succeeds;
In groups the scattering wood recedes,
Hedge-rows, and huts, and sunny meads,
     And corn-fields glance between;
The peasant, at his labour blithe
Plies the hook'd staff and shorten'd scythe:
     But when these ears were green,
Placed close within destruction's scope,
Full little was that rustic's hope
     Their ripening to have seen:
And, lo, a hamlet and its fane –
Let not the gazer with disdain
     Their architecture view;
For yonder rude ungrateful shrine
And disproportion'd spire are thine,
     Immortal WATERLOO!

III

Fear not the heat, though full and high
The sun has scorch'd the autumn sky,
And scarce a forest straggler now
To shade us spreads a greenwood bough;
These fields have seen a hotter day
Than e'er was fired by sunny ray.
Yet one mile on – yon shatter'd hedge
Crests the soft hill whose long smooth ridge
     Looks on the field below,
And sinks so gently on the dale,
That not the folds of Beauty's veil
     In easier curves can flow.
Brief space from thence the ground again,
Ascending slowly from the plain,
     Forms an opposing screen,
With which its crest of upland ground

Shuts the horizon all around
    The soften'd vale between
Slopes smooth and fair for courser's tread: –
Not the most timid maid need dread
To give her snow-white palfrey head
    On that wide stubble-ground;
Nor wood, nor tree, nor bush is there,
Her course to intercept or scare,
    Nor fosse nor fence is found,
Save where, from out her shatter'd bowers,
Rise Hougomont's dismantled towers.

IV

Now, see'st thou aught in this lone scene
Can tell of that which late hath been? –
    A stranger might reply,
'The bare extent of stubble-plain
Seems lately lighten'd of its grain;
And yonder sable tracks remain
Marks of the peasant's ponderous wain,
    When harvest-home was nigh.
On these broad spots of trampled ground,
Perchance the rustics danced such round
    As Teniers loved to draw;
And where the earth seems scorch'd by flame,
To dress the homely feast they came,
And toll'd the kerchief'd village dame
    Around her fire of straw.'

V

So deem'st thou; so each mortal deems,
Of that which is from that which seems:
    But other harvest here,
Than that which peasant's scythe demands,
Was gather'd in by sterner hands,
    With bayonet, blade, and spear.

No vulgar crop was their to reap,
No stinted harvest thin and cheap!
Heroes before each fatal sweep
  Fell thick as ripen'd grain;
And ere the darkening of the day,
Piled high as autumn shocks, there lay
The ghastly harvest of the fray,
  The corpses of the slain.

VI

Ay, look again: that line, so black
And trampled, marks the bivouac;
Yon deep-grav'd ruts the artillery's track,
  So often lost and won;
And close beside, the harden'd mud
Still shows where, fetlock-deep in blood,
The fierce dragoon through battle's flood
  Dash'd the hot war-horse on.
These spots of excavation tell
The ravage of the bursting shell;
And feel'st thou not the tainted steam,
That reeks against the sultry beam,
  From yonder trenchant mound?
The pestilential fumes declare
That Carnage has replenish'd there
  Her garner-house profound.

VII

Far other harvest-home and feast,
Than claims the boor from scythe released,
  On these scorch'd fields were known!
Death hover'd o'er the maddening rout,
And, in the thrilling battle-shout,
Sent for the bloody banquet out
  A summons of his own.

Through rolling smoke the Demon's eye
Could well each destined guest espy,
Well could his ear in ecstasy
    Distinguish every tone
That fill'd the chorus of the fray –
From cannon-roar and trumpet-bray,
From charging squadrons' wild hurra,
From the wild clang that mark'd their way –
    Down to the flying groan
And the last sob of life's decay
    When breath was all but flown.

VIII

Feast on, stern foe of mortal life,
Feast on! But think not that a strife,
With such promiscuous carnage rife,
    Protracted space may last;
The deadly tug of war at length
Must limits find in human strength,
    And cease when these are past.
Vain hope! That morn's o'erclouded sun
Heard the wild shout of fight begun
    Ere he attain'd his height,
And through the war-smoke, volumed high,
Still peals that unremitted cry,
    Though now he stoops to night.
For ten long hours of doubt and dread,
Fresh succours from the extended head
Of either hill the contest fed;
    Still down the slope they drew,
The charge of columns paused not,
Nor ceased the storm of shell and shot;
    For all that war could do
Of skill and force was proved that day,
And turn'd not yet the doubtful fray
    On bloody Waterloo.

IX

Pale Brussels! Then what thoughts were thine,
When ceaseless from the distant line
     Continued thunders came!
Each burgher held his breath to hear
These forerunners of havoc near,
     Of rapine and of flame,
What ghastly sights were thine to meet,
When rolling through thy stately street,
The wounded show'd their mangled plight
In token of the unfinish'd fight,
And from each anguish-laden wain
The blood-drops laid thy dust like rain!
How often in the distant drum
Heard'st thou the fell Invader come,
While Ruin, shouting to his band,
Shook high her torch and gory brand:—
Cheer they, fair City! From yon stand,
Impatient, still his outstretch'd hand
     Points to his prey in vain.
While maddening in his eager mood,
And all unwont to be withstood,
     He fires the fight again.

X

'On! On!' was still his stern exclaim;
'Confront the battery's jaws of flame!
     Rush on the levell'd gun!
My steel-clad cuirassiers, advance!
Each Hulan forward with his lance!
My Guard, my Chosen, charge for France,
     France and Napoleon!'
Loud answer'd their acclaiming shoiut,
Greeting the mandate which sent out
Their bravest and their best to dare

The fate their leader shunn'd to share.
But HE, his country's sword and shield,
Still in the battle-front reveal'd
Where danger fiercest swept the field,
    Came like a beam of light;
In action prompt, in sentence brief,
'Soldiers stand firm', exclaim'd the Chief,
    'England shall tell the fight!'

XI

On came the whirlwind, like the last
But fiercest sweep of tempest-blast –
On came the whirlwind! Steel-gleams broke
Like lightning through the rolling smoke;
    The war was waked anew;
Three hundred cannon-mouths roar'd loud,
And from their throats, with flash and cloud,
    Their showers of iron threw.
Beneath their fire, in full career,
Rush'd on the ponderous cuirassier,
The lancer couch'd his ruthless spear,
And hurrying as to havoc near,
    The cohorts' eagles flew.
In one dark torrent, broad and strong,
The advancing onset roll'd along,
Forth harbinger'd by fierce acclaim,
That, from the shroud of smoke and flame,
Peal'd wildly the imperial name.

XII

But on the British heart were lost
The terrors of the charging host;
For not an eye the storm that view'd
Chang'd its proud glance of fortitude,
Nor was one forward footstep staid,

As dropp'd the dying and the dead.
Fast as their ranks the thunders tear
Fast they renew'd each serried square,
And on the wounded and the slain
Closed their diminish'd files again,
Till from their line, scarce spears' lengths three
Emerging from the smoke they see
Helmet, and plume, and panoply;
        Then waked their fire at once!
Each musketeer's revolving knell
As fast, as regularly fell,
As when they practise to display
Their discipline on festal day;
        Then down went helm and lance!
Down were the eagle banner sent,
Down reeling steeds and riders went
Corslets were pierced, and pennons rent,
        And, to augment the fray,
Wheel'd full against their staggering flanks,
The English horsemen's foaming ranks
        Forced their resistless way.
Then to the musket-knell succeeds
The clash of swords, the neigh of steeds;
As plies the smith his clanging trade,
Against the cuirass rang the blade;
And while amid their close array
The well-served cannon rent their way,
And while amnid their scatter'd band
Raged the fierce rider's bloody brand,
Recoil'd in common rout and fear,
Lancer and guard and cuirassier,
Horsemen and foot, a mingled host,
Their leaders fall'n, their standards lost.

XIII

Then, WELLINGTON, thy piercing eye,
This crisis caught of destiny;
  The British host had stood
That morn 'gainst charge of sword and lance
As their own ocean-rocks hold stance,
But when thy voice had said, 'Advance!'
  They were their ocean's flood.
O thou, whose inauspicious aim
Hath wrought thy host this hoiur of shame,
Think'st thou thy broken bands will bide
The terrors of you rushing tide?
Or will thy Chosen brook to feel
The British shock of levell'd steel,
  Or dost thou turn thine eye
Where coming squadrons gleam afar,
And fresher thunders wake the war,
  And other standards fly?
Think not that in yon columns, file
Thy conquering troops from Distant Dyle –
  Is Blucher yet unknown?
Or dwells not in thy memory still,
(Heard frequent in thine hour of ill),
What notes of hate and vengeance thrill
  In Prussia's trumpet tone?
What yet remains? shall it be thine
To lead the relics of thy line
  In one dread effort more?
The Roman lore thy leisure loved,
And thou canst tell what fortune proved
  That Chieftain, who, of yore,
Ambition's dizzy paths essay'd,
And with the gladiators' aid
  For empire enterprised:
He stood the cost his rashness play'd,

Left not the victims he had made,
Dug his red grave with his own blade
And on the field he lost was laid,
     Abhorr'd – but not despised.

XIV

But if revolves thy fainter thought
On safety, howsoever bought,
Then turn thy fearful rein and ride,
Though twice ten thousand men have died
     On this eventful day,
To gild the military fame
Which thou, for life, in traffic tame
     Will barter thus away.
Shall future ages tell this tale
Of inconsistence faint and frail?
And art thou he of Lodi's bridge,
Marengo's field, and Wagram's ridge!
     Or is thy soul like mountain-tide,
That, swell'd by winter storm and shower,
Rolls down in turbulence of power,
     A torrent fierce and wide;
Reft of these aids, a rill obscure,
Shrinking unnoticed, mean and poor,
     Whose channel shows display'd
The wrecks of its impetuous course,
But not one symptom of the force
     By which these wrecks were made!

XV

Spur on thy way! Since now thine ear
Has brook'd thy veterans' wish to hear,
     Who, as thy flight they eyed,
Exclaim'd, while tears of anguish came,
Wrung forth from pride, and rage, and shame.

'O that he had but died!'
But yet, to sum this hour of ill,
Look, ere thou leavest the fatal hill,
  Back on yon broken ranks
Upon whose wild confusions
The moon, as on the troubled streams
  When rivers break their banks,
And to the ruin'd peasant's eye,
Objects half seen roll swiftly by,
  Down the dread current hurl'd:
So mingle banner, wain, and gun,
 Where the tumultuous fight rolls on
Of warriors, who, when morn begun,
  Defied a banded world.

XVI

List! frequent to the hurrying rout
The stern pursuers' vengeful shout
Tells that upon their broken rear
Rages the Prussian's bloody spear.
  So fell a shriek was none,
When Beresina's icy flood
Reddened and thaw'd with flame and blood,
And, pressing on thy desperate way,
Raised oft and long their wild hurra,
  The children of the Don.
Thine ear no yell of horror cleft
So ominous, when, all bereft
Of aid, the valiant Polack left –
Ay, left by thee – found soldier's grave
In Leipsic's corpse-encumber'd wave
Fate, in those various perils passed,
Reserved thee still some future cast;
On the dread disc thou now hast thrown,
Hangs not a single field alone,

Nor one campaign; thy martial fame,
Thy empire, dynasty, and name,
    Have felt the final stroke'
And now, o'er thy devoted head
The last stern vial's wrath is shed,
    The last dread seal is broke.

XVII

Since live thou wilt, refuse not now
Before these demagogues to bow,
Late objects of thy scorn and hate,
Who shall thy once imperial fate
Make wordy theme of vain debate
Or shall we say thou stoop'st less low
In seeking refuge from the foe
Against whose heart, in prosperous life,
Thine hand hath ever held the knife!
    Such homage hath been paid
By Roman and by Grecian voice
And there was honour is the choice,
    If it were freely made.
Then safely come: in one so low,
So lost, we cannot own a foe;
Though dear experience bid us end
In thee we ne'er can hail a friend.
Come, howsoe'er: but do not hide
Close in thy heart that gem of pride,
Erewhile, by gifted bard espied,
    That 'yet imperial hope';
Think not that for a fresh rebound,
To raise ambition from the ground,
    We yield thee means or scope.
In safety come: but ne'er again
Hold type of independent reign;
No islet calls thee lord,

We leave thee no confederate band
No symbol of thy lost command
To be a dagger in the hand
From which we wrench'd the sword.

XVIII

Yet even in yon sequestr'd spot
May worthier conquest be thy lot
    Than yet thy life has known;
Conquest, unbought by blood or harm,
That needs nor foreign aid nor arm,
    A triumph all thine own.
Such waits thee when thou shalt control
Those passions wild, that stubborn soul,
    That marr'd thy prosperous scene:
Hear this from no unmoved heart,
Which sighs, comparing what thou art
    With what thou might'st have been!

XIX

Thou, too, whose deeds of fame renew'd
Bankrupt a nation's gratitude,
To thine own noble heart must owe
More than the meed she can bestow.
For not a people's just acclaim,
Not the full hall of Europe's fame,
Thy Prince's smiles, thy State's decree,
The ducal rank, the garter'd knee, –
Not these such pure delight afford
As that, when hanging up thy sword,
Well may'st thou think, 'This honest steel
Was ever drawn for public weal;
And, such was rightful Heaven's decree,
Ne'er sheathed unless with victory!'

XX

Look forth once more with soften'd heart,
Ere from the field of fame we part;
Triumph and sorrow border near,
And joy oft melts into a tear.
Alas! what links of love that morn
Has war's rude hand asunder torn!
For ne'er was field so sternly fought,
And ne'er was conquest dearer bought.
Here piled in common slaughter sleep
Those whom affection long shall weep:
Here rests the sire, that ne'er shall strain
His orphans to his heart again;
The son, whom on his native shore
The parent's voice shall bless no more;
The bridegroom, who has hardly press'd
The husband, whom through many a year
His blushing consort to his breast;
The husband, whom through many a year
Long live and mutual faith endear.
Thou canst not name one tender tie,
But here dissolved its relics lie!
O! when thou see'st some mourner's veil
Shroud her this form and visage pale;
Or mark'st the matron's bursting tears
Stream when the stricken drum she hears;
Or see'st how manlier grief, suppress'd,
Is labouring in a father's breast, –
With no enquiry vain pursue
The cause, but think on Waterloo!

XXI

Period of honour as of woes,
What bright careers 'twas thine to close!.
Mark'd on thy roll of blood what names
To Briton's memory, and to Fame's,
Laid there their last immortal claims!
Thou saw'st in seas of gore expire
Redoubted Picton's soul of fire,
Saw'st in the mingled carnage lie
All that of Ponsonby could die,
De Lancey change Love's bridal-wreath
For laurels from the hand of Death,
Saw'st gallant Miller's failing eye
Still bent where Albion's banners fly,
And Cameron in the shock of steel
Die like the offspring of Lochiel;
And generous Gordon 'mid the strife
Fall while he watch'd his leader's life.
Ah! Though her guardian angel's shield
Fenced Britain's hero through the field,
Fate not the less her power made known,
Through his friends' hearts to pierce his own!

XXII

Forgive, brave Dead, the imperfect lay!
Who may your names, your number, say!
What high-strung harp, what lofty line,
To each the dear-earn'd praise assign,
From high-born chiefs of martial fame
To the poor soldier's lowlier name?
Lightly ye rose that dawning day,
From your cold couch of swamp and clay,
To fill, before the sun was low,
The bed that morning cannot know.
Oft may the green and steep,

And sacred be the heroes' steep,
    Till time shall cease to run;
And ne'er beside their noble grave,
May Briton pass and fail to crave
A blessing on the fallen brave
    Who fought with Wellington!

XXIII

Farewell, sad Field! Whose blighted face
Wears desolation's withering trace;
Long shall my memory retain
Thy shatter'd huts and trampled grain,
With every mark of martial wrong,
That scathe thy towers, fair Hougomont!
Yet though thy garden's green arcade
The marksman's fatal post was made,
Though on thy shattered'd beeches fell
The blended rage of shot and shell,
Though from thy blacken'd portals torn,
Their fall thy blighted fruit-trees mourn,
Has not such havoc brought a name
Immortal in the rolls of fame!
Yes, Agincourt may be forgot,
And Cressy be an unknown spot,
    And Blenheim's name be new;
But still in story and in song,
For many an age remember'd long,
Shall live the towers of Hougomont,
    And field of Waterloo.

———

Stern tide of human Time! That knowest no rest,
But, sweeping from the cradle to the tomb,
Bearst ever downward on thy dusky breast

Successive generations to their doom;
While thy capacious stream has equal room
For the gay bark where pleasure's streamers sport,
And for the prison-ship of guilt and gloom;
The fisher-skiff, and barge that bears a court,
Still wafting onward all to one dark silent port;–

Stern tide of Time! Through what mysterious change
Of hope and fear have our frail barks been driven!
For ne'er before, vicissitude so strange
Was to one race of Adam's offspring given,
And sure such varied change of sea and heaven
Such unexpected bursts of joy and woe,
Such fearful strife as that where we have striven,
Succeeding ages ne'er again shall know,
Until the awful term when thou shalt cease to flow.

Well hast thou stood, my Country! The brave fight
Hast well maintain'd through good report and ill;
In thy just cause and in thy native might,
And in Heaven's grace and justice constant still;
Whether the banded prowess, strength and skill
Of half the world against thee stood array'd,
Of when, with better views, and freer will,
Beside thee Europe's noblest drew the blade,
Each emulous in Arms the Ocean Queen to aid.

Well art thou now repaid; though slowly rose
And struggled long with mists thy blaze of fame,
While like the dawn that in the orient glows
On the broad waves its earlier lustre came;
Then eastern Egypt saw the growing flame,
And Maida's myrtles gleam'd beneath its ray,
Where first the soldier, stung with generous shame,
Rivall'd the heroes of the wat'ry way,
And wash'd in foemen's gore unjust reproach away.

Now, Island Empress, wave thy crest on high,
And bid the banner of thy patron flow,
Gallant Saint George, the flower of Chivalry,
For thou hast faced, like him, a dragon foe,
And trampled down, like him, tyrannic might,
And to the gazing world mayst proudly show
The chosen emblem of thy sainted Knight,
Who quell'd devouring pride, and vindicated right.

Yet 'mid the confidence of just renown,
Renown dear-bought, but dearest thus acquired,
Write, Britain, write the moral lesson down;
'Tis not alone the heart with valour fired,
The discipline so dreaded and admired,
In many a field of bloody conquest known;
Such may by fame be lured, by gold be hired:
'Tis constancy in the good cause alone
Best justifies the meed thy valiant sons have won.

It is pointless to compare 'The Field of Waterloo' to his grand narrative poems, for it was a different thing for another purpose. Scott would have thought of himself as a bard, and in 'The Lay of the Last Minstrel' had focused reader attention on the bard to start with, and made his ability to finish his work the key to the whole poem. In subsequent works the reader or hearer had to imagine the bard, or else accept Scott as bard speaking directly through verses intervening between the Cantos. The Gaelic bard had traditionally to give advice to his contemporary audience, usually denouncing creeping modernism which challenged his authority and distanced his patron. Scott made less formal attempt to do this than most of his great contemporaries from Wordsworth to Byron, but he wanted to preach conservation (more than Conservatism) and what he saw as the values it enshrined. 'The Field of Waterloo' must have been the most contemporary of all his imaginative writings (Paul's Letters being essentially factual apart from their exceptionally thin fictional device anent authorship). As such he had new work to do, but he was not going to undertake contemporary work without due respect to the lost loyalties he also conserved. Girt as he was with English precedent victories such as Crecy, Agincourt and Blenheim he judiciously invoked them by invocation of Akenside at the outset, and ended by frankly throwing them over and proclaiming Waterloo as their eclipse. Scotland had been the historic enemy of medieval English invasions of France, and while Scotland and England were officially united by crown (though not yet in Parliament) under Queen Anne during Blenheim Scott's emotional loyalties in that reign respected her half-brother as the true King James VIII, protégé and ally of Louis XIV against whom Blenheim was fought. Waterloo preached three-kingdom unity in and Parliament with Scotland in the forefront by producing its bard, and Ireland by providing its hero. He was facing the future as a Unionist (however much time he would subsequently spend in the past through the anonymous novels). But he wanted his Union to know that it was tripartite, with occasional additional invocations of Wales. And he feared for the survival of the Union as well as for that of Scottish identity if England elbowed the other kingdoms of the archipelago out of public attention or references.

Scott's great poems had been avowedly Lowland as well as Highland in sympathy. So had been the anonymous *Waverley* and so would its successors be.

The idea of the Bard is most famous in Gaelic culture, and it was in that where Scott was most obviously in creative operation in 1815, a year begun by the publication of his last major poem, 'The Lord of the Isles'. He broke from the Bards, and indeed from conventional patriotic poets, in one respect. The Bards wept for their great and little dead in their verse, and he manufactured English-language approximations when necessary. But 'The Field of Waterloo' does more than mourn the dead: it reeks with hatred of war. Scott was not content to show Napoleon as an enemy so great that the achievement of the hero Wellington and his troops, especially Scots, would be correspondingly greater. He could keep Napoleon great by implying this master manipulator in men in thousands was personally somewhat cowardly, and (correctly) belying the rumour that he had charged at the head of his Guards at the close of Waterloo. But the poem actually breaks away from convention in lamenting the loss of the great work Napoleon could have done. His ambition had made him an endless progenitor of war, yet (says Scott) war prevented him from showing his real greatness. Sentiment such as that make 'The Field of Waterloo' a work of greatness in itself.

Naturally it had its work to do particularly in lamenting the deaths of its Scottish heroes, among them Wellington's beloved Lieutenant-Colonel Sir Alexander Gordon (1786–1815), whose brother 1784–1860) George as fourth Earl of Aberdeen would later be Prime Minister during the wretched Crimean War. Dr John Robert Hume (c. 1781–1857), product of Scottish medicine, is our witness (quoted in Rory Muir (Ed.), *At Wellington's Right Hand: the Letters of Lieutenant-Colonel Sir Alexander Gordon 1808–1815* (2003), 405):

> I came back from the battle with Sir Alexander Gordon, whose leg I was obliged to amputate on the field late in the evening. This distinguished officer died rather unexpectedly in my arms, about half-past three on the morning of the 19th; and as I was anxious to inform the Duke as early as possible of the sad event, and was standing at the door hesitating whether ton disturb him or not, Sir Charles Broke-Vere came up to me, and asked me if I knew whether the Duke was awake or not, as he wished (he being quartermaster-general) to take his orders relative to the movement of troops. On this I decided to see if he was awake, and going upstairs to his room, I tapped gently at the door, when he told me to come it. He had, as usual, taken off all his clothes, but he had not washed himself, and as I entered the room, he sat up in his bed, his faced covered with the dust and sweat of the previous day, and extended his hand to me, which I took and held in mine, while I told him of Gordon's death, and related such of the casualties as had come to my knowledge. He was much affected. I felt his tears dropping fast upon my hands, and looking towards him, saw

them chasing one another in furrows over his dusty cheeks. He brushed them suddenly away with his left hand, and said to me in a voice tremulous with emotion, 'Well, thank God! I don't know what it is to lose a battle, but certainly nothing can be more painful than to gain one with the loss of so many of one's friends'.

5

George Gordon Noel, 6th Baron Byron

Byron, as he said in his entrancing unfinished epic *Don Juan* was 'born half a Scot and rais'd a whole one', but with very different circumstances from the secure professionalism which had housed the infant Scott. Whether they found accord on public questions a matter of being Scottish is worth reflection. They certainly agreed on the grandeur of Scottish fidelity to Bonnie Prince Charlie, Byron agreeing with Isaac Nathan (1790–1864) how even starving Scots rejected the reward to be gained by betraying the fugitive prince. Nathan quoted Byron declaring 'that draws forth the highest encomiums on the national character, and is one fine specimen of the retreat of avarice at the approach of integrity' clearly influenced or reinforced by *Waverley* whose authorship he firmly assigned to Scott and thought 'the best novel I ever read' (this being in 1814). He told Nathan that Scott was 'the greatest man of his age' (Nathan, *Fugitive Pieces and Reminiscences of Lord Byron* (1829). Neither Scott nor Byron seem to have been much concerned about their being conservative Tory and radical Whig. In fact their mutual affection dwarfs other considerations.

Byron was still a boy when Scott was rallying support from Buccleuch down to withstand an invasion of Scotland by Napoleon, and as he grew up seems to have chiefly thought of Napoleon as a useful device for getting rid of archaic royalty. ('I wish he would rally and rout your legitimate sovereigns, having a mortal hate to all royal entails' wrote Byron to Tom Moore on 8 January 1814.) But he had enjoyed himself fighting other boys when at Harrow school (1801–05) in defence of Napoleon, specifically in preventing grievous bodily harm to a bust of the Emperor which he bitterly recalled in his Journal on 17 November 1813: 'I am sure when I fought for his bust at school, I did not think he would run away from himself'.

His most formidable contribution to Napoleonic literature 'Ode to Napoleon Buonaparte' was published within a fortnight of Napoleon's abdication and acceptance of empty rule in Elba in April 1814, and the message somewhat resembles Scott's 'The Field of Waterloo' in its reproach to Napoleon essentially for not living up to the greatness of being Napoleon. Scott would seem to have been influenced by it, sharing some of its perception of Napoleon in the light of Milton's Satan opening *Paradise Lost* after his own overthrow. The Satan of Milton's poem is heroic, but grows meaner and more contemptible throughout the epic. Byron also combed Gibbon's *Decline and Fall of the Roman Empire* for an epigraph singling out one of the very last emperors of Rome who had fled to a Dalmatian stronghold rather than resist an inevitable conquest: 'By this shameful abdication, he protracted his life a few more years, in a very ambiguous state, between an Emperor and an Exile'. Byron's 'Ode' itself was youthful, and its author had some way to go before reaching the towering intimacy of Don Juan. But it was certainly memorable, beginning:

I

'Tis done – but yesterday a King!
    And arm'd with Kings to strive –
And now thou art a nameless thing
    So abject – yet alive!
Is this the man of thousand thrones,
Who strewd our Earth with hostile bones,
    And can he thus survive?
Since he, miscall'd the Morning Star,
Nor man nor fiend hath fall'n so far.

2

Ill-minded man! Why scourge thy kind
   Who bow'd so low the knee?
By gazing on thyself grown blind,
   Thou taught'st the rest to see.
With might unquestion'd, – power to save –
Thine only gift hath been the grave,
   To those that worshipp'd thee;
Nor till thy fall could mortals guess
Ambition's less than littleness.

He concluded with a touch of mock-citation of James Thomson (1700–48) and yet at Napoleon's rather than his fellow-Scot Thomson's expense (Thomson being the author of 'Rule, Britannia'):

14

Then haste thee to thy sullen Isle,
   And gaze upon the sea,
That element may meet thy smile,
   It ne'er was ruled by thee!
Or trace with thine all idle hand
In loitering mood upon the sand
   That Earth is now as free!
That Corinth's pedagogue hath now
Transferred his bye word to thy brow.

15

Thou Timour! In his captive's cage
   What thoughts will there be thine
While brooding in thy prisoned rage?
   But one – 'The world was mine';
Unless, like he of Babylon,
All sense is with thy sceptre gone,
   Life will not long confine
That spirit poured so widely forth –
So long obeyed – so little worth!

16

Or like the thief of fire from heaven,
    Wilt thou withstand the shock?
And share with him, the unforgiven,
    His vulture and his rock!
Foredoomed by God – by man accurst,
And that last act, though not thy worst,
    The very Fiend's arch mock;
He in his fall preserv'd his pride,
And if a mortal, had as proudly died!

Byron had intended to leave it there, with Napoleon failing to measure up to the Titan Prometheus and/or Satan and derisive comparisons to Robinson Crusoe, Dionysius the Younger (tyrant of Syracus twice overthrown ultimately resttled in Corinth supposedly as a schoolmaster), Tamerlane (legendarily imprisoning his defeated opponent Bajazet I Sultan of Turkey in a cage) and Nebuchadnezzar of Babylon (Daniel iv. 31–7). If Napoleon had ever read it, he would have been hard put to meet its classical literary citations – especially with Robinson Crusoe (the creation of Daniel Defoe (1660–1731)) finding the footprint, inspired by 'Verses Supposed to be Written by Alexander Selkirk' by William Cowper (1731–1800) whose eponymous real-life Scottish subject (1676–1721) Byron intends readers to recall as imagined in Cowper's lines:

I am monarch of all I survey,
    My right there is none to dispute;
From the centre all round to the sea
    I am lord of the fowl and the brute.
Oh solitude! Where are the charms
    That sages have seen in thy face?
Better dwell in the midst of alarms
    Than reign in this horrible place.

But his publisher John Murray (1778–1843) wrote demanding more stanzas 'to make it more than a sheet and thus avoid the stamp duty' as the admirable Leslie A. Marchand editor of the multi-volume *Byron's Letters and Journals* points out (vol. 4 1814–1815 (1975), 104n). In fulfilment the last ran:

> Where may the wearied eye repose
>   When gazing on the Great;
> Where neither guilty glory glows,
>   Nor despicable state?
> Yes – one – the first – the best –
> The Cincinnatus of the West,
>   Whom envy dared not hate,
> Bequeath'd the name of Washington,
> To make men blush there was but one!

Here Byron did posterity a great service, insufficiently realised, especially in the United States of America many of whose contemporary admirers of Washington (1732–99) might think it blasphemy to have his uniqueness proclaimed by Byron, whose politics and morals some of them would regard as un-American. Byron's point was simple enough. The history of the world was peppered with lives of successful generals who having defeated some menace to their country then assumed supreme power with the aid of an army given its head at the expense of the civilian population. Gaius Julius Caesar (100–44 BC) and Oliver Cromwell (1599–1658) are the most obvious cases in point, but the list is endless. Rome clearly valued traditions of ousting legendary monarchs, limiting emergency dictatorships to six months' rule, revering the memory of Lucius Quinctius Cincinnatus (fl. 458 BC) who having been appointed to defend Rome against the threatening Aequi defeated them and resigned his dictatorship within 16 days. He may not have existed, but his cult was vital to Roman identity, all the more because the last century before Empire had subjected Rome to dictators for life and triumvirs regardless of Cincinnatus. Washington was an obvious candidate for American dictatorship after the British surrender at Yorktown (1781) and the British recognition of their former colonies' independence (1783). Washington left the army and returned to his rural estate. His moral influence played a part in adoption of a new Constitution under which he was chosen as President and reigned from 1789 to 1797, when he returned to his estate. Yet a third time (during the danger of war with a France rapidly passing under the control of Napoleon (1798–99)) Washington accepted the role of commander-in-chief and when the crisis was over, went back to his estate. Whatever the Americans might single out as Washington's virtues (they asserted many and invented more), the world saluted him as the apparently all-powerful thrice leaving the supreme command when the task as commissioned was over. And however weak the final rhyme for 'Washington' Byron was absolutely right in declaring the disgrace to mankind in his uniqueness. In the matter of rhyme, Scott did marginally better in 'The Field of Waterloo' (Stanza XXII) when seeking a rhyme for 'Wellington', partly because he separated the rhyming lines. He had evidently worked that out by close reading of Byron.

Byron supposedly greeted the news of Waterloo 'I'm damned sorry', but the cause of sorrow had begun with the Emperor's extinction in Elba. On Waterloo's eve, 12 July 1815 he had been delighted to receive an abusive letter from a Mr J R, denouncing 'Ode to Napoleon Bonaparte' as being inappropriate in view of Napoleon's resumption of his imperial career with the Hundred Days. In any case J R evidently decided Byron was some English chauvinist hypocrite, to be firmly taken to task: 'Let not Englishmen talk of the stretch of tyrants, while the torrents of blood shed in the East Indies cry aloud to Heaven for retaliation.' Whether or not the suspected J R was Irish, Byron sent it on to Moore: 'I think it will amuse you. The writer must be a rare fellow.' Having got so much pleasure from being misunderstood he evidently decided to misunderstand Napoleon for the benefit of the innocent readers of the radical *Examiner*, where in July he published 'Napoleon's Farewell', purporting to be a translation 'from the French' of Napoleon. Byron shared with his friend Tom Moore and to some extent with their friend Scott a genius for mixing comic with tragic, or at least from being unable to resist its invasion. Having seen his idol fall he evidently decided to pick it up, patch it up, and train it for more appropriate conduct. So he had Napoleon declaim:

1

Farewell to the Land, where the gloom of my Glory
Arose and o'ershadowed the earth with her name –
She abandons me now, – but the page of her story,
The brightest or blackest, is filled with my fame.
I have warred with a world which vanquished me only
When the meteor of Conquest allured me too far;
I have coped with the nations which dreadmme thus lonely,
The last single Captive to millions in war!

2

Farewell to thee, France! – when thy diadem crowned me,
I made thee the gem and the wonder of earth, –
But thy weakness decrees I should leave as I found thee,
Decayed in thy glory, and sunk in thy worth
Oh! For the veteran hearts that were wasted
In strife with the storm, when their battles were won –
Then the Eagle, whose gaze in that moment was blasted,
Had still soared with eyes fixed on victory's son.

3

Farewell to thee, France! – but when Liberty rallies
Once more in thy regions, remember me then –
The violet still grows in the depth of thy valleys;
Though withered, thy tears will unfold it again –
Yet, yet, I may baffle the hosts that surround us,
And yet may thy heart leap awake to my voice –
There are links which must break in the chain that has bound us
Then turn thee and call on the Chief of thy choice!

If this together with its actual author had fallen into the hands of Napoleon it seems moot as to whether he would have burst into tears or demanded that the fraudster be shot. Byron's imagery was far from entirely ribald; around the same time he was working up a lament for a Jacobite killed in the 1745 rebellion, 'Golice Macbane'. Like Scott's, Byron's Waterloo was never too far from Culloden. He tried a few inventions to capture Napoleonic veterans' grief, all 'from the French'. Inevitably there were allusions to Napoleonic veterans who having fought for Napoleon at Waterloo after defecting to the Bourbons were executed by Louis XVIII, notable among them Marshal Ney and Colonel Charles de la Bedoyere. Byron's best pseudo-translation was ready by 26 February 1816 and appeared in the *Morning Chronicle* on 15 March 1816:

Ode
(from the French)

[1.]

We do not curse thee, Waterloo!
Though Freedom's blood thy plain bedew;
There 'twas shed, but is not subnk –
Rising from each gory trunk.
Like the Water-spout from ocean,
With a strong and growing motion –
It soars and mingles in the air,
With that of lost LABEDOYERE –
With that of him whose honoured gfrave
Contains 'the bravest of the brave',
A crimson cloud it spreads and glows,
But shall return to whence it rose;
When 'tis full 'twill burst asunder –
Never yet was heard such thunder
As then shall shake the world with wonder –
Never yet was seen such lightning,
As o'er heaven shall then be bright'ning!

Like the Wormwood Star foretold
By the sainted Sere of old,
Show'ring down a fiery flood,
Turning rivers into blood.

2

The Chief has fallen, but not by you,
Vanquishers of Waterloo!
When the soldier citizen
Swayed not o'er his fellow men –
Save in deeds that led them on
Where Glory smiled on Freedom's son –
Who, of all the despots banded,
With that youthful chief competed?
Who could boast o'er France defeated,
Till lone tyranny commanded?
Till, goaded by ambition's sting,
The Hero sunk into the King?
Then he fell, So perish all,
Who would men by man enthral!

3

And thou too of the snow-white plume!
Whose realm refused thee ev'n a tomb,
Better hadst thou still been leading
France o'er hosts of hirelings bleeding,
Then sold thyself to death and shame
For a meanly royal name;
Such as he of Naples bears,
Who thy blood-bought title bears.
Little did'st thou deem, when dashing
On thy war-horse through the ranks,
Like a stream which burst its banks,
While helmets cleft, and sabres clashing,
Shone and shivered fast around thee –

Of the fate at last which found thee:
Was that haughty plume laid low
By a slave's dishonest blow?
Once – as the Moon sways o'er the tide,
It rolled in air, the warrior's guide;
Through the smoke-created night
Of the black and sulphurous fight,
The soldier rais'd his seeking eye
To catch that crest's ascendancy.
And as it onward rolling rose,
So moved his heart upon our foes.
There, where death's brief pang was quickest,
And the battle's wreck the thickest,
Strew'd beneath the advancing banner
Of the eagle's burning crest –
(There with thunder-clouds to fan her,
Who could then her wing arrest –
Victory beaming from her breast?)
While the broken line enlarging
Fell, or fled along the plain;
There be sure was MURAT charging!
There he ne'er shall charge again!

4

O'er glories gone the invaders march,
Weeps Triumph o'er each levelled arch –
But let Freedom rejoice,
With her heart in hert voice;
But, her hand on her sword,
Doubly shall she be adored;
France hath twice too well been taught
The 'moral lesson' dearly bought –
Her Safety sits not on a throne,
With CAPET or NAPOLEON!
But in equal rights and laws,

Hearts and hands in one great cause –
Freedom, such as God hath given
Unto all beneath his heaven,
With their breath, and from their birth,
Though Guilt would sweep it from the earth;
With a fierce and lavish hand
Scattering nations' wealth like sand;
Pouring nations' blood like water,
In imperial seas of slaughter!

5

But the heart and the mind,
And the voice of mankind,
Shall arise in communion –
And who shall resist that proud union?
The time is passed when swords subdu'd –
Man may die – the soul's renew'd:
Even in this low world of care
Freedom ne'er shall want an heir;
Millions breathe but to inherit
Her for ever bokunding spirit –
When once more her hosts assemble,
Tyrants shall believe and tremble –
Smile they at this idle threat?
Crimson tears will follow yet.

The importance of that impersonation of the French people is
that however admirable the sentiments, the author was still in his
poetic adolescence. The sentiments are important, above all the
concluding equation of Napoleon with the Capet dynasty which
had ruled as much of France as it could for eight centuries and a
half. Linguistic mastery is well on its way, verbal dexterity, bitter
wit educating. The hatred of war is clear, if far below the height
of horror with which he would confront it in Cantos VII to IX of
Don Juan. His marriage had only lasted through 1815. But the
great divide between what poetry Byron was still doing and what

he could do was his actual sight of the battlefield of Waterloo during his visit to Brussels on 3–6 May 1816, for which we may turn back to Pryse Lockhart Gordon's *Personal Memoirs*:

The moment I heard of his arrival, I waited on him, and was received with the greatest cordiality and kindness. 'He had no pleasure', he said, 'equal to that of meeting a friend of his mother's, and of his early age.' I had not seen him for 14 years, when he was at Harrow, at the age of 15. I found much less change in his appearance than there generally is from youth to manhood; the general expression of his countenance had become very like his mother's – a beautiful, mild, and intelligent eye, fringed with long and dark lashes, an expansive and noble forehead, over which hung in dark clusters the rich dark natural curls. What a living representation of [James] Beattie's [(1735–1803)] *Minstrel* [published in two volumes 1771, and 1774 – Byron might have preferred likeness to his friend Moore's 'The Minstrel Boy'].

In our conversation of three hours, he went over the pranks and adventures of his boyish days. He had lived at Banff with his mother for a short time, when he was about seven or eight years of age. My eldest son, of nearly the same age, was his schoolfellow, and he was frequently invited by my brother, the pastor of the town, with whom my boy was living, to pass a holiday at the parsonage: all this he perfectly recollected, and of a tumble he got from a plum-tree, into which he had climbed to get some pears from a wall. 'The minister's wife', said he, 'blabbed to my mother, thinking I might have been hurt; and the old red-nosed doctor, whose name I have forgotten, was sent for, who insisted on bleeding me in spite of screams and tears, which I had at command; for I was a complete spoiled child, as I dare say you know. At last he produced the lancets, of which I had a great horror, having seen them used to bleed my nurse, and I declared if he touched me I would pull his nose. This, it seems, was a tender point with the doctor, and he gave the bleeding up, condemning me to be fed on watergruel, and to be put to bed: these orders I disposed of by throwing the medicine out of the window, and as soon as the doctor had taken his departure, I got out of bed and made my appearance in the parlour. My mother, finding that there was nothing the matter with me, gave me tea and bread-and-butter, which I preferred to brochan – you see I have not forgot all my Scotch.'

He put me in mind of what he called my kindness in lending him a pretty pony, and of my accompanying him to ride in Hyde Park. 'That', said his lordship, 'was 14 years ago, when I came to town to spend the holidays with my poor mother. I remember your pony was very handsome, and a fast galloper, and that we raced, and that I beat you, of which I was not a little proud. I have a wonderful recollection of the little events of my early days, and a warm feeling for the friends of my youth.'

He told me that he was desperately in love with Miss Mary Duff when he was nine years old, 'and we met', he said, 'at the dancing school.' He had many inquiries about her, and if she was still as handsome. 'She is a year older than I am; I have never seen her since I left Aberdeen. Some of the first verses I ever wrote were in praise of her beaity. I know she is happily married, which I rejoice at.' All this he said with much feeling.

As he proposed visiting Waterloo on the following morning, I offered my services as his cicerone, which were graciously accepted, and we set out at an early hour, accompanied by his compagnon de voyage [Dr John William Polidori (1795–1821)]. The weather was propitious, but the poet's spirits seemed depressed, and we passed through the gloomy forest of Soignies without much conversation. As the plan of inspection of the field had been left to me, I ordered our postillion to drive on to Mont St. Jean without stopping at Waterloo. We got out at the Monuments. Lord Byron gazed about for five minutes without uttering a syllable; at last, turning to me, he said – 'I am not disappointed. I have seen the plains of Marathon, and these are as fine. Can you tell me', he continued, 'where Picton fell? Because I have heard that my friend [the Hon. Frederick] Howard [(1785–1815) youngest son of Byron's Chancery guardian Frederick Howard fifth earl of Carlisle (1748–1825)] was killed at his side, and nearly at the same moment.'

The spot was well known, and I pointed with my finger to some trees near it, at the distance of one hundred and fifty yards: we walked to the spot. 'Howard', said his lordship with a sigh, 'was my relation and dear friend; but we quarrelled, and I was in the wrong: we were, however, reconciled, at which I now rejoice.' He spoke these words with great feeling, and we returned to examine the monument of Sir Alexander Gordon, with a broken column, on which he made some criticisms, bestowing great praise on the fraternal affection of his brother, who had erected it. He did not seem much interested about the position of the troops, which I pointed out to him; and we got into our carriage and drove to the Chateau Goumont, the poet remaining silent, pensive, and in a musing mod, which I took care not to interrupt.

The gallant defence of this post seemed to interest him more, and I recapitulated all the particulars I knew of the attack. From the bravery displayed by the handful of troops (the Guards) who defended it, it has acquired its reputation. Though they were reinforced more than once, the number never exceeded twelve hundred, and notwithstanding the enemy had, by battering down the gate of the farm-yard, and setting fire to the straw in it, got possession of the outer works in the evening attack, they could make no impression on the strong-hold the garden

> Whose close-pleach'd walks and bowers have been
> The deadly marksman's lurking screen.

They reaped no advantage by these assaults, on the contrary they sacrificed a great many brave men without any purpose. It was a most important post; for had they succeeded in getting possession of it, and driving out our troops, their guns would have enfiladed us, and we should have been obliged to change our front.

On our return in the evening, I pressed his lordship to dinner, which he declined, saying – 'I have long abandoned the pleasures of the table'. He, however, promised to take his coffee with my wife, provided there was no party. He came at nine o'clock, and greeted her most cordially, again expressing the pleasure he felt in meeting the friend of his mother.

Notwithstanding the interdiction, I had invited two accomplished gentlemen to meet him: one of them, a Hanoverian in ouir service, had travelled in Greece, and being extremely intelligent, a most interesting conversation took place on that classical country which has since so long struggled for its liberties. The poet was in high spirits and good humour, and he charmed us with anecdotes and descriptions of the various countries in the Archipelago and Albania, which he had visited. He neither ate nor drank, and the only refreshment he could be persuaded to take was an ice; but he remained with us till two hours past midnight. My wife exhibited her scrapbook, in which Sir W. Scott had a few months before written a few stanzas on the battle. She begged his lordshipo to do her a similar honor, to which he readily consented, saying, 'if she would trust him with her book, hne would insert a verse in it before he slept'. He marched off with it under his armn, and next morning returned with the two beautiful stanzas which were soon after published in his Third Canto of *Childe Harold*, with a little variation:

Stop, for thy tread is on an Empire's dust.

I consider these as being highly valuable, the primi pensiers of the splendid stanzas on Waterloo.

I asked Byron what he thought of Mr Scott's 'Field of Waterloo' just published – if it was fair to ask one poet his opinion of a living contemporary. 'Oh', said he, 'quite fair; besides, there is not much subject for criticism in this hasty sketch. The reviewers call it a falling off; but I am sure that there is no poet living who could have written so many good lines upon so meagre a subject in so short a time. Scott', he added, 'is a fine poet, and a most amiable man. We are great friends. As a prose writer, he has no rival; and has not been approached, since Cervantes, in depicting manners. His tales are my constant companions. It is highly absurd his denying, what every one that knows him believes, his being the author of these admirable works. Yet no man is obliged to give his name to the public except he chooses to do so; and Scott is not likely to be compelled by the law, for he does not write libels, nor a line of which he need be ashamed.' He said a great deal more in praise of his friend, for whom he had the highest respect and regard. 'I wish', added the poet with feeling, 'it had been my good fortune to have had such a Mentor. No author', he observed, 'had deserved more from the public, or has been so liberally rewarded.'

Lord Byron, in reading aloud the stanzas of Mr Scott,

> For high, and deathless is the name,
> Oh Hougoumont, thy ruins claim!
> The sound of Cressy none shall own,
> And Agincourt shall be unknown,
> And Blenheim be a nameless spot,
> Long ere thy glories be forgot,

exclaimed, striking the page with his hand, 'I'll be d--d if they will, Mr Scott, be forgot!'

The occasion drew together Byron's origins, loves, hates, delights and doom, the conversation on Greece anticipating his own courageous ultimate death to save it.

Did Byron realise these were not the exact words of Scott's poem as published? His memory was excellent, and his facility in elegant and apposite rhyme probably unrivalled. The text was evidently transcribed in 1830 by Pryse Lockhart Gordon from his wife's scrapbook, which means that Scott, like Byron after him, used it for a first draft of an intended high point in the future poem. Scott may have forgotten the exact words and rhymes of his text in the Gordon scrapbook, or have sought to improve them however successfully, but the sentiments are very much the same and we may conclude that first of all Scott had fixed in his mind after seeing Waterloo that here at last was the means of patriotic Union whose tapestry he had been weaving, for England, Ireland, and Scotland, since 'Don Roderick'. On the principle by which his disciple Arthur Conan Doyle would write the Sherlock Holmes stories, Scott thought of the conclusion first and worked his way back. It suggests why the beginning of 'The Field of Waterloo' is flat (as a rude reviewer remarked), but the old fire is in full supply for the last lines of the main text. Pryse Gordon in a footnote acknowledged the source of the lines he quoted on the deadly marksman's lurking screen were also from Scott in the scrapbook, whence Stanza XXIII of the published text of 'The Field of Waterloo' clearly improved:

> Yet though the garden's green arcade
> The marksman's fatal post was made...

As far as Byron's scrapbook text was concerned, Pryse Gordon makes it clear Waterloo had inspired him to resume his *Childe Harold's Pilgrimage* whose first two Cantos had appeared in 1812. They were charming, and youthful. Poetically speaking, Waterloo was making to make a man of Byron. Pryse Gordon was perfectly right. The scrapbook shows that the sight of the battlefield had sent the poet into almost immediate creation, more rapidly and more completely than Scott. Both were romantic poets, but Scott was much more the wizard in control of his creations, Byron more apt to be manipulated by his. The comparable case to Byron at work here would seem to be John Keats (1795–1821) finding a work hitherto unseen by him in the library of a friend, going home, and at once writing 'On First Looking Into Chapman's Homer' which like Canto III of *Childe Harold's Pilgrimage* would be published in 1816. Determined on doing its bit to ensure the immortality of the battle, *Childe Harold*'s Waterloo begins on Canto III, Stanza 17:

17

Stop! – for thy tread is on an Empire's dust!
An Earthquake's spoil is sepulchred below!
Is the spot mark'd with no colossal bust?
Nor column trophied for triumphal show?
None; but the moral's truth tells simpler so,
As the ground was before, thus let it be, –
How that red rain hath made the harvest grow!
And is this all the world has gained by thee,
Thou first and last of fields! King-making Victory?

18

And Harold stands upon this place of skulls,
The grave of France, the deadly Waterloo!
How in an hour the power which gave annuls
Its gifts, transferring fame as fleeting too!
In 'pride of place' here last the eagle flew,
Then tore with bloody talon the rent plain,
Pierced by the shaft of banded nations through;
Ambition's life and labokurs all were vain;
He wears the shattered links of the world's broken chain.

19

Fit retribution! Gaul may champ the bit
And foam in fetters; – but is Earth more free?
Did nations combat to make One submit;
Or league to teach all kings true sovereignty?
What! Shall reviving Thraldom again be
The patched-up idol of enlightened days?
Shall we, who struck the Lion down, shall we
Pay the Wolf homage? Proffering lowly gaze
And servile knees to thrones? No; prove before ye praise!

20

If not, o'er one fallen despot boast no more!
In vain fair cheeks were furrowed with hot tears
For Europe's flowers long rooted up before
The trampler of her vineyards; in vain years
Of death, depopulation, bondage, fears,
Have all been borne, and broken by the accord
Of roused-up millions: all that most endears
Glory, as when a myrtle wreathes a sword
Such as Harmodius drew on Athens' tyrant lord.

21

There was a sound of revelry by night,
And Belgium's capital had gathered then
Her Beauty and her Chivalry, and bright
The lamps shone o'er fair women and brave men;
A thoiusand hearts beat happily; and when
Music arose with its voluptuous swell,
Soft eyes look'd love to eyes which spake again,
And all went merry as a marriage-bell,
But hush! Hark! A deep sound strikes like a rising knell!

22

Did ye not hear it? – No, 'twas but the wind,
Or the car rattling o'er the stony street;
On with the dance! Let joy be unconfined;
No sleepl till morn, when Youth and Pleasure meet
To chase the glowing Hours with flying feet –
But, hark! – that heavy sound breaks in once more,
As if the clouds its echo would repeat;
And nearer, clearer, deadlier than before!
Arm! Arm! And out – it is – the cannon's opening roar!

23

Within a windowed niche of that high hall
Sate Brunswick's fated chieftain; he did hear
That sound the first amidst the festival,
And caught its tone with Death's prophetic ear;
And when they smiled because he deemed it near,
His heart more truly knew that peal too well
Which stretch'd his father on a bloody bier,
And roused the vengeance blood alone could quell
He rush'd into the field, and, foremost fighting, fell.

24

Ah! Then and there was hurrying to and fro,
And gathering tears, and tremblings of distress,
And cheeks all pale, which but an hour ago
Blush'd at the praise of their own loveliness;
And there were sudden partings, such as press
The life from our young hearts, and choking sighs
Which ne'er might be repeated, who could guess
If ever more should meet those mutual eyes,
Since upon nights so sweet such awful morn could rise?

25

And there was mounting in hot haste: the steed,
The mustering squadron, and the clattering car
Went pouring forward in impetuous speed,
And swiftly forming in the ranks of war,
And the deep thunder peal on peal afar;
And near, the beat of the alarming drum
Roused up the soldier ere the morning star;
While throng'd the citizens with terror dumb,
Or whispering, with white lips – 'The foe! They come! They come!'

26

And wild and high the 'Cameron's gathering' rose!
The war-note of Lochiel, which Albyn's hills
Have heard, and heard, too, have her Saxon foes:–
How in the noon of night that pibroch thrills,
Savage and shrill! But with the breath which fills
Their mountain-pipe, so fill the mountaineers
With the fierce native during which instils
The stirring memory of a thousand years,
And Evan's, Donald's fame rings in each clansman's ears!

27

And Ardennes waves above them her green leaves,
Dewy with nature's tear-drops, as they pass,
Grieving, if aught inanimate e'er grieves,
Over the unreturning brave, – alas!
Ere evening to be trodden like the grass
Which now beneath them, but above shall grow
In its next verdure, when this fiery mass
Of living valour, rolling on the foe
And burning with high hope, shall moulder cold and low.

28

Last noon beheld them full of lusty life,
Last eve in Beauty's circle proudly gay,
The midnight brought the signal-sound of strife,
The morn the marshalling in arms, – the day
Battle's magnificently-stern array!
The thunder-clouds close o'er it, which when rent
The earth is covered thick with other clay,
Which her own clay shall cover, heaped and pent,
Rider and horse, – friend, foe, – in one red burial blent!

29

Their praise is hymn'd by loftier harps than mine;
Yet one I would select from that proud throng,
Partly because they blend me with his line,
And partly that I did his sire some wrong,
And partly that bright names will hallow song,
And his was of the bravest, and when shower'd
The death-bolts deadliest the thin files along,
Even where the thickest of war's tempest lower'd,
They reach'd no nobler breast than thine, young, gallant Howard!

30

There have been tears and breaking hearts for thee,
And mine were nothing, had I such to give;
But when I stood beneath the fresh green tree,
Which living waves where thou didst cease to live,
And saw around me the wide field revive
With fruits and fertile promise, and the Spring
Come forth her work of gladness to contrive,
With all her reckless birds upon the wing,
I turn'd from all she brought to those she could not bring.

31

I turn'd to thee, to thousands, of whom each
And one in all a ghastly gap did make
In his own kind and kindred, whom to teach
Forgetfulness were mercy for their sake;
The Archangel's trump, not Glory's, must awake
Those whom they thirst for; though the sound of Fame
May for a moment soothe, it cannot slake
The fever of vain longing, and the name
So honoured but assumes a stronger, bitterer claim.

32

They mourn, but smile at length, and, smiling, mourn:
The tree will wither long before it fall;
The hull drives on, though mast and sail be torn;
The roof-tree sinks, but mokulder on the nhall
In massy hoariness, the ruinmed wall
Stands when its wind-worn battlements are gone;
The bars survive the captive they enthrall;
The day drags through though storms keep out the sun;
And thus the heart will break, yet brokenly lives on.

33

Even as a broken mirror, which the glass
In every fragment multiplies; and makes
A thousand images of one that was,
The same, and still the more, the more it breaks;
And thus the heart will do which not forsakes,
Living in shattered guise, and still, and cold,
And bloodless, with its sleepless sorrow aches,
Yet withers on till all without is old,
Showing no visible sign, for such things are untold.

34

There is a very life in our despair,
Vitality of poison, – a quick root
Which feeds these deadly branches, for it were
As nothing did we die; but Life will suit
Itself to Sorrow's most detested fruit,
Like to the apples on the Dead Sea's shore,
All ashes to the taste. Did man compute
Existence by enjoyment, and count o'er
Such hours 'gainst years of life, – say, would he name three score?

35

The Psalmist numbered out the years of man:
They are enough; and if thy tale be true,
Thou, who didst grudge him even that fleeting span,
More than enough, thou fatal Waterloo!
Millions of tongues record thee, and anew
Their children's lips shall echo them, and say –
'Here, where the sword united nations drew,
Our countrymen were warring on that day!'
And this is much, and all which will not pass away.

Byron had more to say on Waterloo in *Childe Harold* as well as
elsewhere, but time is fleeting, and the threescore and ten neither

of them reached lie ominously in my past. In any case however countless the corpses of Waterloo, its best use may be to introduce more of you to Scott and Byron, or tempt you to renew their friendship, and they are two of the best companions I know, whatever their moods, friends for each other and for us regardless of the ground where we find them. I leave it to you to return to Byron on Napoleon, about whom he reflects in the nest stanzas of *Childe Harold*, and on whom Scott would raise his gigantic historiographical tomb. As for Waterloo, Byron reserved perhaps his ultimate tragicomic epitaph to the beginning of his 'The Vision of Judgment' (1822), a poem which may need a word of explanation. Living in Italy for much of the time since Waterloo may have accustomed Byron to a certain Italianate proprietorial affection for Heaven and its standard personnel. He was genuinely disgusted at the blasphemy of Robert Southey (1774–1843) who, having been appointed Poet Laureate when Scott refused, responded to the death of George III in 1820 with verses depicting the dead King respectfully welcomed into Heaven by suitable predecessors and admirers. Byron responded with a poem of the same name letting George slip quietly into heaven with the implication (probably quite correct) that he had had no intention of causing any harm in any of his deplorable policies. The main business of the poem was to assail Southey as a self-serving turncoat, notably on war: Southey had written a fine satire 'After Blenheim' (1798) in which an old grandfather assures his sceptical infant grandchildren of the magnificence of victory and in so doing brings home its wickedness and folly, only to change or, as Byron's verse put it, 'He had sung against all battles, and again / In their high praise and glory'. And the theme of hatred of war was proclaimed by Byron's poem at the outset:

I

Saint Peter sat by the celestial gate,
His keys were rusty, and the lock was dull,
So little trouble had been given of late;

Not that the place by any means was full,
But since the Gallic era 'eighty-eight',
The devils had ta'en a longer, stronger pull,
And 'a pull altogether', as they say
At sea – which drew most souls another way.

2

The angels all were singing out of tune,
And hoarse with having little else to do,
Excepting to wind up the sun and moon,
Or curb a runaway young star or two,
Or wild colt of a comet, which too soon
Broke out of bounds o'er the ethereal blue,
Splitting some planet with its playful tail,
As boats are sometimes by a wanton whale.

3

The guardian seraphs had retired on high,
Finding their charges past all care below;
Terrestrial business filled nought in the sky
Save the recording angel's black bureau,
Who found, indeed, the facts to multiply
With such rapidity of vice and woe,
That he had stripped off both his wings in quills,
And yet was in arrear of human ills.

4

His business so augmented of late years,
That he was forced, against his will, no doubt,
(Just like those cherubs, earthly ministers)
For some resource to turn himself about,
And claim the help of his celestial peers,
To aid him ere he should be quite worn out
By the increased demand for his remarks,
Six angels and twelve saints were named his clerks.

5

This was a handsome board – at least for heaven;
And yet they had even then enough to do,
So many Conquerors' Cars were daily driven,
So many kingdoms fitted up anew;
Each day too slew its thousands six or seven,
Till at the crowning carnage, Waterloo,
They threw their pens down in divine disgust –
The page was so besmear'd with blood and dust.

6

This by the way, 'tis not mine to record
What angels shrink from: even the very devil
On this occasion his own work abhorr'd,
So surfeited with then infernal revel,
Though he himself had sharpen'd every sword,
It almost quench'd his innate thirst of evil.
(Here Satan's sole good work deserves insertion –
'Tis, that he hath both generals in reversion.)

The very gentleness and languid humour, tricked around with all the providence of a resourceful teller of fairy tales to children, made the ferocity of the blows all the harder once Byron began to punch.

In that same year of 1822 Byron resumed work on his *Don Juan*, a charming narrative perpetually interrupted by sardonic, wise and humane philosophy. But on the lessons of Waterloo it best summed up in Canto VII, Stanza 41, lines 1–2:

'Let there be light', said God, and there was light!
'Let there be blood', says man, and there's a sea!

Epilogue

The Bonnie Bunch of Roses

There is a folk ballad sung throughout the 19th century in many versions, and printed by widely-scattered presses in varying forms, making it popular across the length and breadth of the United Kingdom. Its anatomy upon diagnosis yields formations and symptoms indicating antecedents in Ireland, England and Scotland. Its parentage is Jacobite, its conclusions are Unionist, but it has a faintly Napoleonic coda. Its unreality has brought problems to librarians who are uneasy in fixing it too directly on Napoleon I as a subject, while its reappearances at many points in mid-century have prompted erroneous topical ascription to Napoleon III (1808–73). Its protagonist is in fact Napoleon II (1811–32) who made such little actual impact on history that even his life in fantasy is bibliographically overlooked. I have used several divergent texts including my Cork-born mother's version sung to me as a child: I doubt if she ever saw it written down until long afterwards. It has been printed under such titles as 'Young Napoleon; or The Bunch of Roses':

> By the dangers of the ocean,
>   One morning in the month of June,
> These finely-feathered warbling songsters
>   Their notes so sweetly sang in tune,
> There I espied a female
>   Seemingly in grief and woe,
> Conversing with young Bonaparte
>   Concerning the Bonnie Bunch of Roses O!

O then spoke young Napoleon,
   And grasped his mother by the hand,
'Dear Mother, pray have patience
   Until I'm able to command;
I will raise a terrible army
   And through tremendous dangers go,
And in spite of all the universe
   I will gain the Bonnie Bunch of Roses O!'

'When first you saw great Bonaparte,
   You fell upon your bended knee,
And asked your father's life of him,
   He granted it most courteously.
'Twas then he took an army,
   And o'er frozen realms did go,
He said "I'll conquer Moscow,
   And gain the Bonnie Bunch of Roses O!"

'He took three hundred thousand men,
   And likewise kings to join his throng,
He was so well provided,
   Enough to sweep the world along;
But when he came to Moscow,
   He was overwhelmed by the driven snow,
Moscow was a-blaze,
   And he lost the Bonnie Bunch of Roses O!

'But if I live to take command,
   St Helena's rocks will shake,
Its castles, walls and palaces,
   All for my aged father's sake.
With courage bold undaunted
   I'll save Napoleon from his foes,
And in spite of all the universe
   I will gain the Bonnie Bunch of Roses O!

'Oh, mother, he was loyal,
　　And always he proved true to you,
Until that fatal morning
　　He saw the plains of Waterloo.
He left numbers that lie on the ground,
　　And blood in fountains there did flow,
And Grouchy proved a traitor,
　　And he lost the Bonnie Bunch or Roses O!'

'Now, son, ne'er speak so venturesome,
　　For England's is the Heart of Oak,
England, Ireland and Scotland,
　　Their unity will ne'er be broke,
And think of your brave father,
　　In Saint Helena his body lies low,
And you will follow after,
　　So beware the Bonnie Bunch of Roses O!'

'Oh, Mother, adieu for ever!
　　Now I am on my dying bed,
If I had lived I should have been clever,
　　Now, I droop my youthful head,
Yet while our bones do moulder
　　And weeping willows o'er us grow,
The deeds of bold Napoleon
　　Will sting the Bonnie Bunch of Roses O!'

The most obvious Scottish contribution to 'The Bonnie Bunch of Roses' is its fairly obvious affinity for bagpipe music, of the style with which the Gordons and Greys and Black Watch may have improved Waterloo. The English element may be the Roses, although individual Irish roses supplied patriotic symbols as in 'Roisin Dubh', translated many centuries later by James Clarence Managn (1803–49) floridly as 'Dark Rosaleen', though the better translation of the title is 'The Little Black Rose' – which was used for an apparently original poem by Aubrey de Vere (1814–1902) and further appropriated by Joseph Mary Plunkett (1887–1916) for another original poem. All of the poems are ambiguous as to whether their prime moving spirit is erotic or patriotic, Ireland being the object of the patriotism. De Vere's first line and Plunkett's full title 'The Little Black Rose Shall be Red at Last' assert the theme of metaphorical recolouration. The most famous Scottish patriotic use 'The Little White Rose of Scotland' is by Hugh MacDiarmid aka Christopher Murray Grieve (1892–1978), its clothing erotic. These cases suggest very old usages of roses for tribal inspiration, making the identification of Union with the bunching of individual, national roses. But the bunching process is English, given the 15th-century dynastic battles where the conflicting cousins of Lancaster and York represented themselves as Red and White Roses, and were declared to be United by the marriage of Henry VII Tudor (1457–1509, rgd from 1485) to Elizabeth of York (1466–1503). Whoever framed the poem was using the unification of England to include roses from Ireland and Scotland (the latter being whatever original Scottish rose MacDiarmid had in mind).

However, the poem opens in classic Jacobite style, Irish in custom, Scottish in subject, English in awareness that Jacobite reconquest would be final only when all three kingdoms accepted the Stuarts. June was the month of Waterloo, but the Irish *Aisling* common pattern is otherwise carefully followed. The poet sees a weeping lady who turns out to be Ireland, mourning her departed prince, whether James VII and II (1633–1701, rgn from 1686, ousted 1688) or his son James 'VIII and III' (1688–1766), or his other (illegitimate) son James 'Fitzjames', the Marshal Duke of Berwick (1670–1734) who could really qualify for proto-Wellington heroic status. Sometimes the poet comforts her with news that the absent hero would soon return, although occasionally he might declare the hero dead. The possible alternative identities of the exiled king or one or other of his sons feeds in to the 'Bonnie Bunch' with its two Napoleons. What it cannot do, *pace* librarians, is to alternate as far as Napoleon III, since the assumptions of a Napoleonic challenge to the 'Bonnie Bunch' is that the United Kingdom will always be his enemy, whereas Napoleon III became the friend of the UK, fought alongside it in the Crimean War, and took refuge in it when expelled from France in 1870 after defeat in the Franco-Prussian War. The full text of the ballad demands composition after Napoleon II's death in 1832, but it cannot be later than 1848 when Napoleon III began his rise to power. The cult of the exiled Stuarts was always at its strongest in Scotland, and Bonnie Prince Charlie was thus a precedent for the hope that a heroic son might redeem the cause in which his father had failed.

This accords agreeably with Walter Scott's acceptance of Waterloo as the true Unionist martial credential. He was never going to support Napoleon, but he accorded with the 'Bonnie Bunch' in certainty that the Union was at last an honourable refuge for Jacobites, whether because their leaders ultimately – tacitly or explicitly – made George the Prince Regent and later King their heir, or because Waterloo ended any possibility of Napoleon as alternative Jacobite inheritor. The great Glaswegian historian of France, Professor Denis Brogan (1900–74), in his book *The French Nation 1814–1940* (1957) instinctively linked Jacobite and Napoleonic returns in hope for restoration, while contemptuous enough of their absurdity:

> The adventure which a Royalist official was soon to christen 'the Hundred Days' was one of the most reckless and disastrous gambles of modern history. Compared with it, the 'Forty-Five was almost defensible. (p. 12.)

Walter Scott instinctively linked them as well, but without Brogan's advantage of knowing the inevitability of Waterloo. He had feared a Napoleonic invasion of Scotland during the Bonapartist high tide; he even antedated that fear and roused his audience with its alarm when concluding *The Antiquary* (1816), and his disciple Arthur Conan Doyle introduced him in a cameo in his romance *The Great Shadow* (1892), which culminated in Waterloo. The ironies were falling thick and fast on Scott's head in the Hundred Days, since he had just published his immortal story of the '45, *Waverley* (1814) featuring Prince Charlie at his most attractive, and for all of his personal distaste for Napoleon he of all men knew how electric the native response to a returned claimant to a national throne could prove. But between him and the 'Bonnie Bunch' we have enough evidence to show that however much Enlightenment might preen itself on the wisdom of the Union under which it flourished in Scotland, Romanticism helped establish the tripartite Union in the minds of its peoples and it did so by enlisting Jacobite traditions and security fears in Waterloo.